Warwick Forge is currently Director of the Victoria Conservation Trust. A former assistant administrator of the National Trust of Australia and trained as a lawyer he appeared regularly on behalf of the Trust at conservation and planning hearings. Before leaving the Trust in 1983 he became involved in the first rumblings of the Wade house case and maintained an active interest in it thereafter. He is a former commissioner of the Australian Heritage Commission and is well known in Victoria for his involvement in conservation and town planning issues. He lives in the inner Melbourne suburb of North Carlton.

GW00726059

The royalties from the sale of this book will be donated to the South Parkville Preservation Fund.

First published 1985
by McCulloch Waterloo Press
723 Elizabeth Street, Waterloo, NSW

© Warwick Forge, 1985

Designed by Guy Mirabella
Typeset by ProComp Productions Pty Ltd, Adelaide, SA
Printed by W. Brooks & Co, Waterloo, NSW
ISBN 0 949048 32 1

Front cover cartoon by Peter Nicholson first appeared
in the *Age*.

The Wade House Case

Warwick Forge
Foreword by Sir Rupert Hamer

McCulloch Waterloo Press

Chronology of Events

1972
June   South Parkville classified as an Historic Area by the National Trust.

1981
May   Council dismissed and replaced by three Commissioners.
Sept.   The Wades purchase 17 Fitzgibbon Street from Alfred Palmer for $130,000.
Nov.   Notini and Chisholm sign their 'consents' to Wade's plans.
1 Dec.   Application to Melbourne City Council by Day (for the Wades) for a planning permit for extensions and renovations to the rear of the house.
Christmas Eve   Council determines to grant the permit.

1982
28 May   Wades commence demolition of front balcony and wing walls.
29 May   Neighbours learn of front proposal and express disapproval to Wades when they gather in street.
2 June   Day gives 'architectural lecture' to residents who then discover rear extensions. Fresh plans appear mysteriously on Council file.
6 June   Seven bricklayers complete front brick fence without permit. Next day, Wade meets with Bethke at the Town Hall.
23 June   Wades, via Day, apply for permit for front fence and façade.
26 June   Day and Lewis publish their competing architectural views on the front of the house in the *Age*.
June–July   Respective solicitors canvass possible compromise settlements.
7 July   Trenches dug in readiness to pour foundations for extensions.
19 July   Despite assurances, Wades build beyond disputed area to first floor.
22 July   Residents informed that Council would commence proceedings to revoke rear permit and Council deleted as a defendant from the writ at suggestion of City Solicitor.

0 July	Writ and summons for an injunction issued while builders work overtime and at weekends.
3 Aug.	Gobbo J declines to commence injunction hearing, assures residents that their position will not be prejudiced and orders summons to be set down for 'earliest possible date in September'.
6 Aug.	Gobbo J hears challenge by Wades against Council revocation proceedings. Council wins with costs awarded against Wades.
2 Aug.	Revocation of permit hearing for rear on grounds of mis-representation before Commissioners which results in resolution not to revoke permit.
Sept.–Oct.	Council joined as a defendant to the writ. Wades join Day as a defendant seeking indemnity from him.
8 Nov.	Order for speedy trial granted for rear hearing.
16 Nov.	Ombudsman advises that he can no longer investigate the matter owing to service of the writ.
23 Nov.	Wades appeal to Appeals Board concerning Day's plans for façade and front fence following Council refusal to grant permit. Hearing adjourned till May 1984.
Dec.	Wades successfully prosecuted by Council for works to the façade without a permit. Wade placed on 6-month good behaviour bond and required to pay costs of $418.40.
Dec.	Cain Government removes Commissioners and restores elected Council.
Dec. 82–Nov. 83	Supreme Court action concerning the rear fixed in various lists but never reached.

1983

10 Feb.	Miss Chisholm dies.
July	Wade prosecuted by Council for constructing trellis fence without permit. Placed on one month good behaviour bond.
Oct.	Council resolves to hand matter over to insurers.
Nov.	Supreme Court hearing concerning the rear commences before O'Bryan J. and runs for 24 days.
9 Dec.	O'Bryan delivers oral judgement in favour of residents on 'main issue' of validity of permit but they fail to obtain a remedy, are therefore unsuccessful and must bear most of the costs.

1984

9 Mar.	O'Bryan delivers revised written reasons for judgement.
May	Planning Appeals Board hears appeals concerning the front fence and façade (4 days).
7 June	Council deputation meets with their London insurers.
7 July	Planning Appeals Board delivers its determination adverse to the Wades.

28 Aug.	Council deputation meets with Simmonds, Minister for Local Government, seeking Government support to solve the problem concerning the rear.
19 Dec.	Bethke and Murray meet with Walker, Planning and Environment Minister, to seek Government legislation enabling Council to assist residents.

1985

7 Mar.	Full Court appeal commences concerning rear (9½ days) Judgement confirms O'Bryan judgement on 21 May.
22 Mar.	Bethke and Murray brief D. Whittington, (Premier's Adviser on Wade case explaining how Government can resolve case and how such resolution would not be a precedent.
25 May	Colebatch feature article, the *Age*, 'A legal dispute worthy of a Dickensian plot'.
13 June	Democracy in Planning Group formed at meeting at Clunies Ross House under Chairmanship of Professor John Power.
20 Aug.	Council resolves to pay compensation provided the Government passes the requisite enabling legislation.
Oct.	Wades commence work to façade in accordance with Appeals Board determination.
30 Oct.	The *Age* reports that Premier Cain has decided to become involved in resolution of the Wade case concerning the costs aspects.

Contents

Author's Note

Wherever possible, I have sought to reduce legal jargon to a minimum. Thus the term 'residents' is employed rather than 'plaintiffs', 'objectors' and 'appellants'. In relation to the rear of the house, the plaintiffs were Dr and Mrs Thorne, Mr and Mrs Forsey, Dr and Mrs Brown, Dr Falk, Mr Notini and Miss Chisholm. With regard to the front, there were over thirty residents who were 'objectors' but the most active were Dr Thorne, Mr Frank Barrington and Dr Jack McCrae. 'Council' replaces 'responsible authority' and instead of the cumbersome, 'false representations and misrepresentations', I simply use, 'misrepresentation'. 'Planning Act' replaces 'The Town and Country Planning Act, 1961'.

Foreword

This modern cautionary tale, told with passion and deep concern by Warwick Forge, unfolds inexorably like a latter-day Greek tragedy to its appointed ending in disappointment and injustice. It demonstrates how a serious error of judgement by a public authority (the Melbourne City Council) in granting a building permit for restoration of a Parkville property without giving other affected parties a chance to object, involves two quite innocent groups—the Douglas Wades as building owners, and the nearby residents—in acrimonious and lengthy legal proceedings, in which the residents win their legal point, but are left with enormous legal bills for costs to meet, which will compel them to sell the very homes they were trying to protect.

Warwick Forge was deeply involved himself in what he plainly regards as a travesty of planning principles—law without justice—and he unravels the tangled story with great skill and clarity. It is not necessary to adopt all his strictures on the legal systems and sundry judges of the Supreme Court of Victoria to perceive that there is something very wrong in our planning procedures which can allow a group of residents innocently setting out to protect their properties against a highly detrimental development, and successfully obtaining a court declaration that the building permit was invalidly granted, to be left with the development in place and crippling bills to pay for the legal costs of all parties.

How could such injustice happen? In the clear vision of hindsight, it is obvious that there were mistakes all round in a situation which confused many people, and where clear precedents and guidelines did not exist.

The true value of a powerful and affecting study like this, however, is not to apportion blame, but to illuminate the problem and seek ways of preventing any repetition. It is clear that the courts, with their complex procedures, their inevitable delays, and their very high costs, are not the most effective instrument for obtaining prompt decisions on planning matters, where speed is likely to be of the essence. Indeed in this very case, it was the long delay in reaching a legal decision which precipitated most of the problems.

The author canvasses certain solutions. I would prefer to

1

see a rapid procedure developed to enable the Planning Appeals Board to deal expeditiously (and cheaply) with disputed planning permits which involve failure to give notice to potential objectors. For a time, that Board allowed itself to become far too legalistic and formal (contrary to its original charter) but more recently it has shown welcome signs of being more accessible to ordinary citizens concerned about planning decisions. Even more important, any planning authority which makes a serious error (as in this case), which involves two other innocent parties in costly litigation, must be given the power and duty of meeting the costs which flow from its error.

That is not the case today. This book explains how the planning process, which has had outstanding success in achieving orderly growth and in protecting both our architectural heritage and the amenity of ordinary citizens, can sometimes go seriously awry. Indeed, there are actually two stories in the book: one, in which the planning process worked rapidly and justly; the other, in which it signally failed to achieve either speed or any kind of just result.

The Planning Appeals Board must make itself even more accessible to ordinary citizens and even more considerate of their interests.

Above all, the Board must strongly repel the attitude of some, which emerges in this book, that objectors are ill-intentioned ratbags who have to be silenced by aggressive legal tactics. Objectors will often by misinformed, and often motivated principally by self interest but the Board is perfectly capable of sifting fairly the various views presented to it without unwarranted legal histrionics.

The book would not fulfil the purposes of its author if it did not generate a real and widespread public demand for reform, as well as for some measure of compensation for the unwitting victims of a defective Act, as commonsense and true compassion clearly require. I hope it does, and so will all enlightened readers of this study.

·Rupert Hamer
October 1985

Introduction

If ever there was a case which showed up the deficiencies of the court system, this is it.

A lawyer for the residents[1]

There seems to be something sinister about this whole case.

Professor Carrick Chambers[2]

On 5 January 1982, the Melbourne City Council Commissioners granted a permit for extensions to the rear of Mr and Mrs Doug Wade's home at 17 Fitzgibbon Street, South Parkville.

This action precipitated extraordinarily protracted efforts, both legal and otherwise, to have the permit reviewed and the development made subject to the normal town planning appeal processes. Ultimately, the Supreme Court was to hold the permit null and void and a 'disaster' for residents to the south.

Despite this, local residents obtained no relief from the impact of the illegal building and have instead been lumbered with the vast majority of the legal costs—approximately $650,000! The Wades have also suffered both personally and financially and must surely regret the day they set foot in the district.

Most of the Melbourne City Councillors believe that the residents should receive financial relief because it was the Council Commissioners who issued the invalid permit and then failed to revoke it. However, they do not have the legal power to assist and Councillors have been personally threatened with litigation should they speak out about the matter.

The State Government has been accused of callous indifference because it has failed to facilitate a settlement and consistently refused to acknowledge any moral responsibility. The Premier John Cain appears to believe that once a matter has gone to court then that is the end of it, regardless of the fact that the whole problem would never have arisen but for the Government's defective legislation and the failure of Government appointed Commissioners to revoke the permit. The Government has ignored the deficiencies of the judicial processes and has been oblivious to the manifestly unjust results.

Was it then a clash between differing values and aspirations — on the one hand Wade saying that the locals were university academics living in a 'cocoon with no idea of the real world', and on the other, residents claiming that the Wades were using steamroller tactics and ignoring the local community entirely? Ultimately in planning terms, the debate largely focusses upon the rights of the individual as opposed to those of the community. In that context, the role of the Melbourne City Council was critical.

Should the individual be permitted to do whatever he likes with his castle, and how should the responsible body resolve these conflicting interests?

In the present case, the residents were aggrieved by the proposed extensions at the rear and took the matter up with the Wades, the Council and everyone they could get to listen to them. This was to no avail with the result that the residents were compelled to seek legal action. The Wades said their permit was valid, the residents said it was not. The Council eventually announced proceedings to revoke the permit (which would have required the Wades to make a fresh application subject to the normal surveillance and objection procedures) and everyone breathed a sigh of relief. The residents sought an injunction to halt further building and to protect their position but failed. Nevertheless, the judge provided them with an assurance that their position would not be prejudiced, since he said that if the Wades continued to build, then they did so at their own peril.

The Commissioners failed to revoke the permit after Doug Wade had responded to Commissioner Smith's request to look him in the eye and to say he was innocent of misrepresenting the plans to his two elderly neighbours. Construction raced ahead, the parties failed to reach agreement and negotiations broke down. Fifteen months later, when the residents finally got the matter into court, the Wades had finished construction. Although the permit was eventually held to be invalid, the judge decided that the Wades had proceeded in good faith, were innocent of misrepresentation, had not taken a 'calculated risk' and accordingly he was not prepared to require the Wades to pull the extension down.

This book will not be welcomed by lawyers, bureaucrats and politicians. The entire case has been infused with bureaucratic intransigence and indifference on the one hand and a reactionary legal system—which is too slow, too expensive and too bogged down with its own procedures—on the other. The manifest injustice of this case and the horrendous costs imposed have sparked off a wave of criticism and disenchantment with the legal profession which in turn has reacted defensively. Even the *Age* newspaper has been targeted for angry responses by the legal establishment.

Today many people sincerely believe that a grave injustice has been perpetrated and support has been forthcoming from right across the political spectrum, from former Liberal Premier, Sir Rupert Hamer, to ALP State President, Gerry Hand.

The question that residents pose time and again but which remains unanswered is: what should the ordinary citizen do in the face of an unlawful development next door which will result in substantial detriment to his property? What more could the residents have done in this case?

The final decision now rests with the State Government. Will it be responsive and accept some moral responsibility? Will it at least allow the Melbourne City Council to compensate the innocent victims? A tragedy it certainly is, since the residents have been financially ruined through no real fault of their own and most will have to sell the very homes they sought to protect in order to meet the massive legal costs.

Obviously eventually the law must and will be changed. The community simply will not stand for permits being unlawfully issued without such decisions being capable of review expeditiously and at reasonable cost. Public bodies must be accountable for their misdeeds and we must recover that 'tradition of 800 years of independent courts standing as guardians of the individual against the great power of government'.[3]

This is a true horror story. It is also a tale of quite heroic efforts by civic-minded families to uphold the law and pursue justice for themselves and their disadvantaged neighbours. It is amazing to think that it could happen again at any time, to you or to me or any homeowner in Victoria who seeks to protect his home by calling a halt to wrongful actions by a Council or the illegal works of a neighbour which may prove, as the judge was to find, a 'disaster'.

It may be said that this is a one sided tale and that I have seen the story solely through the eyes of the residents. This is largely true in the sense that my concern all along has been to focus on the problems of ordinary law-abiding people who somehow became enmeshed in the legal machinery.

I have, however, tried to be objective although the task has been made difficult given a lack of co-operation in some quarters. Twice I sought to speak to the Wades — once at the outset of the case and again while working on this book. On both occasions I was rebuffed. The second time, Doug Wade said, 'You are just a joke mate. You had an affront to ring me and also to write me a letter' — and then hung up! Unfortunately, too, the Town Clerk has continued the tradition of non-information by forbidding me access to the Council's files and to the City Solicitor, Ian Murray, who had till then been quite prepared to talk with me. For some time, too, senior government spokesmen refused to discuss the matter in any detail.

On a more positive note, I have had the benefit of wide ranging discussions with most of the barristers involved — save for those representing the Wades — and this has proved of inestimable value although their views diverge sharply in relation to most of the key issues. For professional reasons these people must remain anonymous and I cannot acknowledge their assistance personally.

The litigation proved to be very complex and to chart some novel and treacherous waters. It should be clearly understood

6

that I make no personal criticism of any of the lawyers involved. As Justice O'Bryan was to comment, 'It is a relatively simple matter to judge an issue with hindsight'. Garth Buckner, QC, has said that Neil Brown, QC, though the loser, did a splendid job and I have absolutely no doubt that the whole clutch of legal gladiators (about a dozen in all) threw themselves into the forensic contest with all the energy at their disposal.

At times I seriously wondered whether I had the qualifications for writing this book at all when much of the discussion inevitably focusses upon the law. I have not practised as a lawyer although I have a law degree and have had experience in the town planning and environmental law fields. I did not anticipate the complexity of the subject at the outset, but I was encouraged to doggedly stick at it because I believed it was a tale worth telling and because it also seems to me that sometimes outsiders, like Charles Dickens and Tim Colebatch, have something useful to say about the machinations of the law.

Ultimately, it is the moral issues which are the most arresting. In this regard, the Melbourne City Council has come full circle and has reached a point of accepting its responsibility to make some reparation to the parties. The State Government on the other hand, has consistently shirked the issue and in so doing failed to protect the innocent or to respect the concept of justice inherent in our planning system.

Inevitably, occasional errors of fact may have crept into the text despite my best endeavours and I would appreciate advice where corrections are in order. As to the opinions expressed, I take sole responsibility, knowing full well that many readers will strongly disagree with them. But that is the nature of this case.

The purpose of this book then is to highlight the struggles and endeavours of ordinary, innocent people and in this way, to press for reform of an inadequate legal system and for a fair and just settlement of this legal nightmare.

Footnotes

[1] Like most lawyers, this one chose not to disclose his identity.

[2] Professor Carrick Chambers, Professor of Botany, University of Melbourne.

[3] Michael Kirby, *Reform the Law*, OUP, Melbourne, 1983, p. 177.

1
Origins of the Dispute and the Planning Context

One of the most tragic circumstances that I think can occur in regard to decision making of a local government and planning type . . . it continues to be a tragic set of circumstances . . . The matter is so complex and difficult that I should not like to place blame . . . I should indicate that on no occasion has the State Government seen itself as in any way involved directly with the problem, and it would have been incorrect in taking part and would still be so because the matter is still subject to legal action.

The Hon. Evan Walker, Minister for Planning[1]

When Dr Miles Lewis, the prominent architectural historian, rang me on the morning of Sunday 30 May 1982, about some problem in Fitzgibbon Street, Parkville, I reluctantly agreed to inspect the property—more because of my regard for him than from any premonition that I might be projected into the most controversial, convoluted and tragic urban dispute of its kind in Australia's history.

At first blush the Wade house case seems straightforward. A well known football personality buys a house in an inner suburban area near his business interests. He engages an architect to design alterations for the building and obtain the necessary permits. The brief resulted in a 'flat front' (and therefore removal of the front verandah), a high front fence and major rear extensions.

Number 17 Fitzgibbon Street, South Parkville, was purchased by Doug and Raelene Wade in September 1981 for $130,000 from a Mr Palmer, who in the 1950s had enclosed the front verandah, removed the decorative cast iron and replaced the ground floor front window and door.

South Parkville is an attractive inner suburban residential

The front of the Wade house with work halted. Following warnings from the Council, Wade was prosecuted for building without a permit and work ceased for two and a half years until October 1985 when it re-commenced in conformity with the Appeal's Board Determination.

17 Fitzgibbon Street as it was in 1945.

area close to the University of Melbourne, to parks and to the city. From the late sixties the area started to enjoy something of a revival and its intact Victorian streetscapes attracted the attention of the National Trust's first Metropolitan Historic Area classification. Shortly afterwards, the Premier Sir Rupert Hamer, returning from an overseas trip, enthusiastically declared that South Parkville and other such areas should be preserved through planning controls.

Local residents recognised the historic value of the area and researched the history of all 350 dwellings. They were proud of their precinct and its history and they recognised the aesthetic and other advantages which accrue with the sympathetic restoration of the dwellings.

Ten years later, when the Wade house controversy began, people moving into the area who wished to renovate their homes were usually aware or were informed by their architects that planning controls existed. Permits were required which theoretically reconciled the rights of the individual with community planning objectives.

The major dispute which this book describes concerns the extensions to the rear of the building and the validity of the permit issued to architect Norman Day. That the plans for alterations to the front were held by the Planning Appeals Board to be inimical to the conservation of the area was a quite separate issue. Initially work to the front had proceeded without a permit. Wade was warned and then prosecuted by the Council when he persisted. Thereafter, the matter was dealt with in conformity with the normal planning procedures. However, in relation to the rear extensions, the primary concern of the residents throughout was that the development should not be above the law and that the permit should be subject to the normal review processes.

The problem at the rear was first recognised at 7.30 a.m. on 7 July 1982, when Giovanni Notini, who lived at number 19, rushed in to Dr and Mrs Thorne at number 11. He was greatly distressed having just discovered workmen in his garden demolishing his rear side wall. The Thornes' concern for their elderly Italian pensioner neighbours was relayed to Miss Chisholm and to Mr and Mrs Forsey who lived at numbers 15 and 13 respectively, to the south of the development. Dr Barbara Falk, who lived in Benjamin

Street to the rear of the building, became involved at a later stage.

Neither the Thornes nor Falk had any significant personal or financial interest in the matter. They did, however, believe that being good neighbours required them to assist the elderly, the infirm and people like the Notinis—Italian pensioners who speak little English.

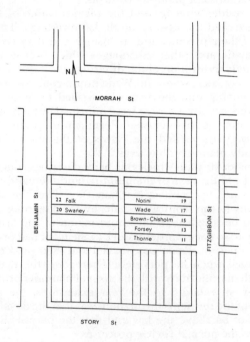

Plan of residents' houses showing relationship to the Wade house.

Personalities

In all, seven residents and their families were to become chief players in this epic struggle.

Dr Peter Thorne, 45, lives with his wife Kay and two teenage children at 11 Fitzgibbon Street. They have lived in that street for nearly thirty years. He is a computer scientist and university lecturer and she is the Administrator of the Royal Australian Chemical Institute. They chose their present house because it was bigger than their previous one and because of its large rear garden. Peter Thorne maintains a strong professional and personal interest in the relationship between technology, science and people. This leads him into areas such as computers for the handicapped, work in prisons and the problems of people coping with technological change. Kay Thorne has maintained a lower profile throughout the ordeal though she has had frequent occasion to display her fund of common sense. While her husband is remarkable for his relentless lateral thinking, Kay is the sheet anchor.

Sidney and Lorretta Forsey have lived at 13 Fitzgibbon Street for about ten years. He is a clinical psychotherapist. They have an unusual capacity to create an ambience of repose around them and to visit their home is to feel one's anxieties and tensions begin to melt. They are garden lovers who enjoy spending time outdoors and have industriously landscaped their back garden. Lorretta Forsey suffers from rheumatoid arthritis and consequently needs the sun for therapy. They built a solarium at the rear of their house to catch the sun—a place for peace, deep thought and comfort. Sid Forsey has been able to provide a special perspective on the events; he sought to bridge the gap between the contestants who distanced themselves from one another, thereby preventing constructive dialogue and possible settlement of the dispute. Both the Forseys felt deep concern for the fate of Mr and Mrs Notini and the late Miss Chisholm. Forsey wrote to the Wades at an early stage of the controversy:

> I know that I would not be happy unless *both* parties feel some satisfaction with the outcome, otherwise bitterness and resentment can continue for years . . .
>
> *I would like to feel comfortable with both of you as neighbours, and I would like for you to feel comfort and peace when living at No 17.*
>
> The first step in achieving this, I have learnt, is to tell you as clearly as I know how just what I want in this matter. If you agree that your wants are similar to mine, then I would be happy if we could at least meet and share this amount of agreement. If you

> would like to take the next step as well (which would involve
> exploring possible mutually satisfactory outcomes), then I would
> try to get Dr Peter Thorne (the spokesman for the residents) to
> be present. (author's italics)

This letter was met with an abrupt response from the Wades'
solicitor indicating there was no point in discussion. Forsey
would sit for days in court preparing detailed notes, at times
analysing the judges involved. He detested the adversarial
system and what he saw as the destructive nature of the courts.

Dr Ken and Mrs Helen Brown are in their early forties and
live at number 15, immediately south of the Wades. They are
the ones who have suffered most from the sheer southern wall
of the extensions to the north of their rear garden. She is a
librarian and they have one child, Rowan. Their lives appear
to have been overwhelmed by the litigation and their appre-
hension for the future. Their health has been consistently
poor. They purchased the house, a 'renovator's opportunity'
(that is, in need of urgent repair), but their meagre funds
have vanished in legal fees and they are now in deep financial
trouble. They are clearly the major victims in terms of physical
and psychological stress. The Browns bought their home
from Miss Chisholm in March 1982. When they came to
appreciate the problem of the Wades' development in June,
they concluded that Miss Chisholm had acted in good faith
and decided to honour the spirit of their contract as well as
their legal obligations with her. The decision has cost them
dearly in both human and financial terms.

At 19 Fitzgibbon Street, Giovanni and Marina Notini live
quietly. Notini has been aghast at the legal process: 'It is like
somebody kills my son', he says. 'You go to court, they say,
"You can serve six years in prison for bringing this to court".'

Giovanni Notini is a retired toolmaker who fought with the
anti-fascist partisans in Italy and came to Australia in the late
forties. He has difficulty speaking English although his comprehension is good. He has a passion for opera and used to
love to lie in his hammock in the sun in his rear garden.
Marina Notini is shy and at the commencement of the controversy was overcome with a nervous rash. She withdrew
into herself and now avoids mixing with people. Once a
happy woman with a ready laugh she is now timid and
frequently depressed.

Miss Chisholm, who sold her boarding house to the Browns, was in her seventies and faced her problems resolutely with quiet conviction. From the outset her solicitor cautioned her against involvement in the litigation. But her resolution in that regard was shattered at the injunction hearing when, with the Notinis, she heard Wade's account of how he had described the development to them when he obtained their consent to the plans. It was not in accord with their recollections and their dismay was such that they thereupon agreed to be joined as parties to the action. Unfortunately, Miss Chisholm died prior to the litigation.

Dr Barbara Falk is the wild card in the pack. She is a highly respected and much loved figure at the University of Melbourne, where she was the former head of the Department of Advanced Education. An indomitable although diminutive figure, she is utterly steadfast in her principles. She purchased her home in Benjamin Street, directly behind the Wade house, for her retirement. Ironically she bought it from someone who had wanted to construct a second storey extension which had been prohibited on planning grounds. Dr Falk agreed to be involved when architect Norman Day gave what he described as an 'architectual lecture' to the residents.

Doug Wade is well known for his brilliant football career as a full forward for Geelong and as a sports commentator. Although he has complained bitterly about his reception in Parkville and has obviously suffered financially, outwardly he seems to have shouldered the problem of living in an environment where people are opposed to his views and style. But inevitably he, too, must have suffered. His architect, Norman Day said this of him:

> I think Doug Wade is a champion person. He was, and remains, one of our folk heroes in football lore and is admired as an honest and true man. He is also tough and willing to fight for something he believes in. This case highlights those qualities. When most people may have relented to pressure from a misguided group, Doug Wade maintained a presence and decency.[2]

Raelene Wade described the experience as '. . . the most traumatic two years of my life. I walk out the front door, there is a continuous parade of people . . . there have been busloads of kids and their teacher said, "Look at what the Wades are doing".'[3]

She always appears as a well-dressed, handsome and confident woman but her reported comments have been rare. One exception was a letter published in the *Age* on 3 July 1982:

HOUSING CHOICE
from Mrs Doug Wade

I refer to our house in Parkville.

Why did we demolish the built-in verandah we inherited upon purchasing the building? Simply because we chose to.

Why did we not replace the 'lacework' that wasn't there at the time of our purchase? Simply because we chose not to.

However, we have chosen to replace the existing metal-framed post-war picture window with others more complimentary to Victorian architecture.

Why did we not replace the picket fence that didn't exist? Once again, simply, we chose not to.

Instead, we chose a high brick wall similar to the many others guarding Victorian terraces in Parkville, Carlton, East Melbourne and all over the world for that matter.

Why in this country, Australia, must we explain our choice?

R. Wade
Parkville

The Wades employed Norman Day as their architect because he was known to them as the *Age*'s architectural critic and because he was recommended by a friend. He had obtained considerable publicity through his provocative articles. It is said that with the death of Robin Boyd, Day sought to establish himself as the heir to Boyd's unrivalled position in architecture. In recent years he has won architectural awards for his post-modernist buildings. In his early articles he displayed a sensitivity to the environment and on one occasion he deplored the practice of buildings being adorned with a single letter motif. It was therefore intriguing to note that his plan for the Wades' house had a large W emblazoned on the façade.

Many observers believe Day created more problems than he solved. In any event, he has also been touched by the tragedy of this case. When I last saw him he seemed to have aged rapidly and clearly his practice has suffered as a consequence.

The Town Planning Context

Town planning in Victoria is controlled by the Town and Country Planning Act of 1961. In the metropolitan area, planning permits are required for most building works and as in the present case, consideration may need to be given to whether a permit is required under the Melbourne and Metropolitan Planning Scheme as well as the Melbourne City Council's Interim Development Order.

Should a resident object to a Council's decision to grant a permit, there will normally be an appeal to the Planning Appeals Board. The Board has had a somewhat chequered history. Originally, when the Act was passed in 1961, appeals were heard by the Minister personally. Eventually, the need for a permanent quasi-judicial body became apparent and the Planning Appeals Board was formed (originally as the Town Planning Appeals Tribunal). Its chief architect, Sir Rupert Hamer, recently described its *raison d'être:*

> It was indeed intended to ensure that ordinary people could attend as objectors before the Town Planning Appeals Board and be heard in person, without the trappings and expense of legal representation, and that the Appeals Board should be able to make a fair and reasonable decision without being bound by strict legal rules of evidence, since opinion and personal feelings, as well as aesthetics, may well be vital elements in a particular case.[4]

During the sixties and seventies, when Melbourne was booming with development, the Board (Tribunal) gained a reputation for being pro-development and susceptible to the arguments of high-powered barristers. Despite the fact that economic and financial factors were supposed to be irrelevant, many historic buildings were demolished during the sixties and the face of Melbourne changed considerably. At the 1973 CBA Banking Chamber Inquiry, Rodney Davidson, Chairman of the National Trust, tabled a copy of *Early Melbourne Architecture*, which established that since the book was published in 1953, more than half of the superb city buildings depicted had been demolished or were in serious danger of demolition.

Gradually, people came to appreciate that some very unpleasant things were happening to Melbourne. Too many fine and historic buildings had been lost. Too many disasters had occurred, like Princes Gate Towers which drastically affected what was arguably the State's most important vista along St Kilda Road towards St Paul's Cathedral. Rodney Davidson announced the 'Battle for the City' and in due course the Collins Street Defence Movement was formed and this came to be spear-headed by the successful and articulate architect, Evan Walker.

In 1976, with the State Government's approval, the Council rushed through its own planning control over demolition. It was simply, if not crudely worded, and provided no criteria for whether or not a building should be demolished. However, at least a start had been made and for the first time bodies like the Trust and the Collins Street Defence Movement could validly object to proposed demolitions.

The next major event was the dismissal of the Council in May 1981 and its replacement by three Commissioners. This decision was largely in response to growing criticisms that the Council was inactive and lacked direction. Certainly the Council had been in a complete dither over what to do about historic buildings and had frequently agreed to their demolition.[5]

Despite these difficulties, the impetus to fight for the city had gathered pace and the Collins Street Defence Movement was replaced at the time of the Council sacking by Melbourne Voters Action, which acted as the Council watch-dog. Future Councillors like Trevor Huggard, Winsome McCaughey and Ewan Ogilvie fronted up to the Appeals Board hearings with National Trust representatives to protest at demolitions and weigh in on wider planning issues. They were confronted by barristers acting for developers who had a habit of using legalistic phrases and arguments laced with in-house jokes, making the layman feel uncomfortable and disoriented.

A number of Board members were unsympathetic and could barely conceal their impatience with resident activists. Some were also uninformed about many town planning, conservation and amenity issues.

Applications for demolition, with one minor exception, were never refused, to my knowledge, and at one stage I was reported in the *Age* as saying that the Trust was losing about 90 per cent of cases before the Appeals Board and that it was virtually a waste of time attending.

The New Deal

In 1982 the Cain Labor Government swept to power. It seemed like the dawn of a new age. It introduced the charismatic Evan Walker as Minister for Planning and Conservation, an established Labor Party policy supporting resident and conservation action, and gave a firm assertion that metropolitan conservation areas would be created. Part of the Labor Party's election platform advocated community participation:

> Modern government requires the creative input of an active voluntary conservation movement. It is imperative that decision making processes related to environmental issues, include as a matter of course the involvement of groups and individuals who are keenly aware of those issues . . . legal standing in appeals has been denied. A Labor Government in Victoria will increase financial and legal assistance to such bodies, and ensure legal standing.[6]

It was, however, some time before the winds of change penetrated the fusty corridors of the Appeals Board. One day the Chief Chairman, Phil Opas, QC, at a luncheon for the Building Owners and Managers Association, naïvely and savagely attacked the concept of preserving historic buildings in the city of Melbourne.

The Premier, John Cain, reacted swiftly, demanded his resignation and when this was not forthcoming, negotiated an agreement by which Opas was banned from personal involvement in cases which concerned historic buildings. No doubt there were many ways in which the Board's attitudes came to be influenced by new government initiatives but I doubt whether anything had such a dramatic effect as the Opas outburst and the swift response. Another significant development was the appointment to the Board of fresh faces like Dr Renate Howe, Stuart Morris and Ian Marsden.[7]

Attitudes at the bar, however, were even slower to change and a handful of barristers were well known for their lack of sympathy for conservationists. None was so formidable in the minds of residents and conservationists as Garth Buckner, QC, who seemed to act for every major developer in the State. A highly emotional, relentless barrister, he could strike terror into the hearts of many witnesses and laymen. One of his tactics was to harass them by challenging their right to be heard and to threaten punitive costs. I do not think this was so much malevolance on his part as a passionate drive to succeed and to do the best he possibly could for his client. (Away from the forensic struggles, he can be great company discussing his pet subjects of period films and football.) At one stage Buckner showed a certain elation when a member of the Carlton Association appealed to the Board and had costs of $2000 awarded against him. In an article headed, THAT'LL LARN EM! Buckner had this to say:

> In every day and age, there are a group of people who, by a process of self-election, appoint themselves as guardians for others. In the town planning field, many of these people can be found in so-called 'conservation' groups. Unfortunately, Governments of whatever persuasion in this State, have allowed such persons to object to developments, without incurring any risk as to costs. Whilst there are arguments that this situation should be allowed to exist, there can be no doubt that in some instances the position is abused . . .[8]

It was in this context of change that the Wades' proposals were to be considered. Government, planners and the community generally were adjusting to a new era in which conservation planning was being taken seriously and freedom of information, accountability of public bodies and similar trends in the legal/planning world were well under way.

The problems associated with the front of the Wade's house were less attenuated so let us deal with them first.

Footnotes

[1] *Hansard*, 7 May 1985.

[2] Letter to the author, 27 September 1985.

[3] The *Age*, 9 February 1985.

[4] Letter to the author, 18 June 1985.

[5] To be fair, the Government had failed to dispose of the compensation bogey (that is, the belief that the Council might be liable for refusing an application to demolish), which meant that councils were terrified of being sued and it was not until the Cain Government came to power that the law was quickly amended to remove this potential threat.

[6] *Conservation and Planning*, Australian Labor Party, 6 March 1982. Issued by Evan Walker, then shadow Minister for Planning.

[7] Ian Marsden was in fact appointed by the previous Thompson (Liberal) Government.

[8] *Town Planning Information and Research Service*, no. 83/84-79, published by Garth Buckner. To be fair, it should be noted that in the particular case (Appeal no. P83/1442) there was only one objector, a Mr R. A. Cunningham, who lodged the appeal but did not appear at the hearing which must have caused the applicant, New Lincoln Inn Hotel, real inconvenience and expense.

2

The Front of The House, Historic Conservation and the Planning Appeals Board

> But the case is also important to Parkville residents, the Council and the public at large as it is the first major case in which urban conservation controls have been closely analysed.
>
> *Determination of the Board*

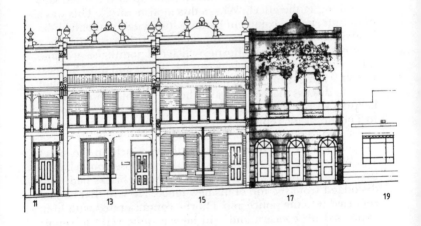

A working drawing for the renovations; the fence is not shown. Courtesy the *Age*.

On Saturday 29 May 1982, workmen were on site at the front of the Wades' house and they explained to local residents that the balcony and wing walls of the house were to be demolished and that a high brick wall was to be constructed at the front. Although the neighbours were not well informed on Council planning policies, they knew that these proposals were contrary to the spirit of conservation for the area, and that high brick walls were usually forbidden. They also knew that other residents were generally required to restore their homes sympathetically.

Doug Wade arrived in his vehicle to find a number of neighbours discussing the work in the street. He subsequently emerged from his house with a copy of the plans which he showed to the residents. He explained, according to the residents, that it was proposed to restore the building. At one stage an outspoken Irishwoman, Annie Oakes, who had recently restored her house in nearby Morrah Street, came up to Wade and said something to the effect, 'What's this monstrosity?'. This was a most unfortunate comment because it inevitably offended the Wades. It transpired at the Supreme Court hearing that they confused her with Kay Thorne, which did nothing to promote the prospects of dialogue between the Wades and the Thornes! In fact, Thorne rang Wade the next day and asked if they could meet to discuss the issue because he felt the plans were out of keeping with the area and might not be authorised. According to Thorne, Wade replied, 'No. I have all the necessary permits and I think you people have a nerve'.

A week later the Wades stopped their vehicle in the street and Wade called out to Thorne, 'Well, I suppose you're happy now'. He was referring to the fact that some bricks had been dislodged from the top of his new fence. He said that he had reported it to the police and Thorne commiserated with him, expressed his concern and said he was quite right to report the matter. Thorne discussed the more general problem and said he was concerned at the difficult position Wade had got into. He invited the Wades in for coffee. Wade seemed on the point of accepting the invitation; he turned to his wife and hesitated for a moment and Thorne repeated the invitation, saying the coffee had been freshly brewed. Wade then said he really had to go, at which point Thorne said, 'The invitation stands for another time'.

However, there has been no other time. Thorne still believes that this was a lost opportunity. Thereafter, the Wades showed no desire to hold discussions with the residents and negotiations through solicitors failed to yield results.

Doug Wade instructed Norman Day to meet with the residents to try and resolve their queries concerning the proposals. Day suggested providing the residents with what he described as an architectural lecture. There were about twenty residents who met at the Thornes' home on 2 June to hear the architect speak. Day showed slides of buildings—mostly of Palladio and Michelangelo designs in Italy—which he said had provided him with his inspiration to re-design the Wades' house. He then showed his plans for the front which indicated a high brick fence with a curving indentation for a gate and for works to the façade of the house which included demolition of the balcony and the protruding wing walls.

The residents pointed out that the plans did not bear a permit stamp, to which Day replied that they were a copy of the endorsed plan which was at his office. Debate then ensued, with the residents stating that they had inspected the plans at the Town Hall and that they did not indicate any works to the façade or construction of a front fence. Eventually, the President of the South Parkville Community Planning Group, Dr Jack Lynch, said, 'You are wasting our time, Norman. On Monday you brought no drawings; today you bring drawings without permit stamps. I have also seen the Council permitted plans, they are not the same as these'. Day maintained they were the same.

I shall never forget that moment. Lynch had never had contact with Day prior to this confrontation but he did not pull any punches.

DR LYNCH: I believe . . .[1] [that is not the case]. Why not get your drawings which you say are the same as these and permit stamped? Why not get them now?
MR DAY: I don't want to go back to my office now.
DR LYNCH: I will drive you myself. Come on, let us get them and settle this.
MR DAY: Oh, I do not want to go back now.

The Day proposal, stripped of its verandah and wings walls—
inspired by Palladio and Michelangelo—cause of the first
controversy. Courtesy Norman Day.

The conversation became heated and I intervened, saying we were getting nowhere and that the best solution would be to visit the Town Hall the following day to resolve the matter. This suggestion was adopted by Day and the residents. However, just after 9.00 a.m. the next morning, Day rang me and said that he would not come because to do so would be contrary to legal advice he had obtained. I was puzzled by this as I could not imagine why a lawyer would advise him against inspecting plans at the Town Hall. In any event, I inspected the endorsed plans at the Town Hall and found that Lynch had been correct and that Day's statements were wrong. There was no permit for works to the façade or for a front fence. There was, however, another set of plans indicating proposed works to these areas, and I was told they had only been lodged on the afternoon of the previous day! Subsequently at the hearing, Day was asked about these plans which bore his name and presumably came from his office. He said that he had not lodged them nor had anyone from his office.

To return for a moment to the meeting at the Thornes' residence. Day had told us that he sympathised with our objections to the front fence and that he was confident that Wade would agree to a traditional picket fence since he was a 'reasonable man'. He said that until the problems concerning the front were clarified work would be halted. Before leaving he gave us a copy of the plans.

After he left, some of the residents noticed what appeared to be extensions to the rear. I was employed at the National Trust at the time and our concern was with the historic character of the area; as far as I was concerned, what went on at the rear seemed of little consequence to my interests. I merely glanced at the rear section and left the meeting.

Two days later, seven bricklayers started to build a cream brick fence approximately two metres high in front of the Wades' house. Knowing that the work lacked a permit, the residents were incensed. The media was contacted and when I arrived on the scene there were three camera crews filming the work. A dozen or so neighbours had gathered. I was amazed. I had never seen a fence rise so rapidly. Doug Wade appeared and was obviously acutely embarrassed, hurrying inside without stopping to talk to reporters.

The media covered the story. I was contacted by the newspapers and was quoted as saying something to the effect that the work being done was 'illegal', which was true enough. This coupled with the subsequent Council intervention may have enraged Wade. In any event I was told that Garth Buckner, QC, had been engaged and that 'proceedings would be taken against an officer of the Trust . . . early next week'. The comment was obviously directed at me and presumably referred to defamation.

Rodney Davidson, chairman of the Trust, had annotated my report 'We will support you. Keep me advised'. Fortunately the writ was never issued but it provides a clue to the intense feelings aroused at the time. I do not think I have ever known a case where such hostility developed in response to resident action.

Apparently someone, though not one of the residents, contacted Norm Gallagher, Secretary of the Builders Labourers Federation, who announced a holding ban on further work 'to allow the problem to be sorted out'. Two days later, on 10 June, the *Sun* reported that Big Norm had relaxed the ban because Wade had rung and assured him that the building was not classified by the National Trust. The Council formally advised the Wades that permits were required and work finally ceased at the front of the building. However, by this time the fence was up, demolition of the façade was almost complete and the windows had been rebuilt in 'neo-Georgian Dayism'. In due course, Council officers recommended to the Council Commissioners that permits be granted for the façade alterations and the front fence, but after an inspection the Commissioners refused to grant the permit. The Wades then appealed to the Planning Appeals Board and the residents knew that they were in for a hearing in order to preserve their historic area.

The decisions of the Commissioners not to issue permits for the front façade and fence were given in September and November 1982. However, because Supreme Court proceedings were already under way concerning the rear of the house, the Wades chose to resolve those issues first. Consequently, the Appeals Board granted an adjournment with the consent of all parties and the actual hearing concerning the façade and fence did not commence until 1 May 1984.

'. . . when Mr and Mrs Wade arrived outside the house to inspect the works a hostile crowd gathered to protest the desecration of an important part of the streetscape.' (Justice O'Bryan) The 'hostile' and 'uncompromising' crowd demonstrate, but to no avail. The illegal construction of the fence races ahead.

Stuart Morris, chairman of the Planning Appeals Board.

Doug Wade in his heyday as full forward for Geelong.
Courtesy the *Age*.

The Hearing

On the whole, the hearing and results were excellent. In the first place, the decision was a landmark for historic conservation issues and secondly, the time and costs expended on the case were perfectly reasonable.

Day had prepared plans displaying a façade stripped of its verandah balcony and wing walls and decorated with a large frieze adorned with vines, bananas and pineapples. It may help to illustrate the impact of the design if it is pointed out that the pineapples were intended to be almost as large as whole windows. There were also changes to the windows and door with which the preservationist would cavil.

Many of the arguments canvassed were novel, sophisticated and seductive and it is a great tribute to the Board that the determination emerged with such a complete and rigorous grasp of the issues. It was, as the Board observed, 'the first major case in which urban conservation controls have been closely analysed'.

The Chief Players

The Appeals Board was presided over by Stuart Morris as its Chairman. He had been selected by the Minister, Evan Walker, because of his capability and background in conservation and planning issues. At the start of the hearing Morris had not yet turned 34 and his selection for the task proved a fitting tribute to an outstanding career. He had won both the Supreme Court and Archibald law prizes in 1974 and had become a senior member of the Board in 1983. Along the way he had been active in local government and conservation issues and served as Sherbrooke Shire President in 1978–79.

Although the determination bears all the hallmarks of his handiwork, Morris was ably assisted by the experienced engineer Alan Kinder. Rita Avdiev, a former architect, was the third member. After some procrastination, she dissented and delivered a minority determination.

The Council had not felt it necessary to brief a barrister but was well served by solicitor Ian Murray, who had thoroughly prepared his case. He had recently returned from a trip to London flushed with enthusiasm for conservation of historic buildings.

Murray was ably supported by the irrepressible Dr Miles Lewis as an authority on conservation and architecture. As the best architectural historian in the country, Lewis was eminently qualified.

The National Trust was represented by the earnest and industrious Craig Porter, while the Wades had Tom Neesham who had recently become a Queen's Counsel. Neesham is an Englishman who had been the Deputy Ombudsman and chaired a government police enquiry during his time at the bar. In mid 1985 he became a County Court judge.

Neesham laboured before the Board in a self-righteous manner. Nor were the Wades well served by Norman Day, their architect, since time and again he got himself into difficulties giving evidence.

The residents represented themselves, luxuriating in the freedom of being able to say their piece without fear of punitive legal costs. Peter Thorne, Frank Barrington, Mark Duckwork and Jack Lynch all presented submissions but it was Thorne who had the greatest impact. With his well presented case he made several telling points. However, the residents' case was not assisted by Ken Brown's appeal over the rear trellis fence, which was a trivial matter and should have been abandoned.

Norman Day had described his intentions in an article in the *Age* to which Miles Lewis contributed a sister article outlining his objections to Day's proposal. Day said.

> My proposal was to strip away the tatty garbage on the front of the house and create a new façade with the classical decoration of late-Victorian architecture — not literally but inventively. The design calls for three new arched door/windows at ground level, exactly like those on other terraces in Parkville . . . echoing the Victorian original . . . Over these Victorian windows I propose a low frieze mural of garlands, vines and other late-Victorian decoration which is like that on the Benvanatu [sic] Mansion in Carlton — a building which has just been fully restored by the National Trust. The façade and fence is to be richly ornamented and finished with the same grey cement wash as the rest of the wall which would give it a 'quiet' and respectful character, like Benvanatu [sic].[2]

However, when the hearing commenced on 1 May, fresh plans were brought forward (the Board taking a 'dim view' of the lack of notice), which involved a cast-iron palisade fence, deletion of the frieze mural, window boxes and an entrance canopy. The fence had a curved indentation to the gate. The Board did not quite agree with Day's claims, and pointed out that the new arched doors and the upper windows were not really similar to others in the Parkville area. Some time was spent with expert witnesses, discussing the style of the proposal. The Board concluded:

He [Day] said that it was not a restoration, although it was reminiscent of the Victorian era. This had been achieved by using pseudo-historic architectural details from various periods in a way which, although drawing on the past, does not accurately reflect the buildings of any particular era. One expert witness described the proposal as emulating a Georgian or neo-Georgian style. The Board believes this description is as close to the mark as one could get, although it might be more apt to describe the proposal as post-modernist. There is one matter, however, upon which all agree. The proposed façade and fence is *not* a restoration.

Thus the battleground was marked out. Day's approach was both forceful and subtle. He produced a 'design criteria' justifying his design and relying upon the *Burra Charter*, a technical document which sets out restoration standards for the guidance of professionals. For example, Article 18 states: 'Reconstruction is limited to the completion of a depleted entity and should not constitute the majority of the fabric of a place'. This, he claimed, provided an ethical and intellectual bar to replicating the original façade. He had, as the Board noted, been more 'colourful' in his article in the *Age*:

Now, it seems, some of the neighbours and their advisers don't like our ideas. They argue that the house should be re-made as a Mickey Mouse recreation of its neighbours, a museum piece rather than an interpretive [*sic*] recreation.

I do not agree with them and I think history does not support their view . . . the residents' blinkered approach to architecture reminds me of philistines in our community who think all art in a gallery should be old, at least 100 years old, to be important. They would prefer forgery of the old types to real creative originals.

I do not believe Parkville must be rebuilt as a boring Disneyland museum based on a book of rules and I don't trust those who advise these people that there is only one way to make buildings suit an historical environment.

To my way of thinking the people who oppose this proposal have been badly advised to a point where they favour caricature or artistic forgery rather than creative Victorian-style architecture.

The Board examined Day's 'design criteria' in detail and concluded:

The Board feels bound to say that Day's document is *misleading and disingenuous*. The document omits the most crucial recommendations in the 'action plan', which relate to demolition and restoration, and selectively quotes various other recommendations relating to the building elements in restoration. One of the headings used in Mr Day's document was titled 'Building elements in restoration' and this seems to imply that, at least in 1982, Mr Day regarded his creation as a restoration, albeit an inventive one. When he gave evidence before the Board, however, Mr Day took a new tack. He told the Board that, not only was his design not a restoration, but that restoration was not possible because of the provisions of the *Burra Charter*.[3] (author's italics)

It is of interest that the Board referred to Lewis' evidence as 'illuminating'. I suspect that it was as favourably impressed with Lewis' article in the *Age* as it was unimpressed by Norman Day's evidence and that its understanding of the whole case was greatly advanced as a consequence. Lewis' attack had been mercilessly accurate. 'The present confrontation was deliberate', he said. And of Norman Day:

...that prominent architectural marverick... it was a marvellous opportunity for a witty cocking of the snoot at a culturally rich environment... For this is what post-modernism in architecture is about . . . taking established architectural traditions and inverting or distorting them, and about responding in an unexpected way to the context in which the building is to stand.

It is in associating himself with Palladio and Michelangelo that Day commits the ultimate hubris, for the work shows a lack of sensitivity for the past. What he has produced is tawdry, insensitive gimmickry.

For once Day's wit and clever convoluted arguments proved inadequate to sway the Board. Nevertheless, he still managed to win a few laughs. One cannot but admire his brilliant, albeit superficial response when asked whether he regarded the Wade house as 'historically important'. He quickly responded, 'It is, NOW!'

The Decision

> If we had lost this one it would have meant the end for all the conservation areas.
>
> *Jack McCrae, President, Parkville Association*

The decision proved a major victory for Parkville and for conservation in general. The majority decision was given by Stuart Morris and Alan Kinder in a carefully worded thirty-three-page determination. Their primary findings were:

• The area had been recognised for its special character over a lengthy period. It was not significant because of individual architectural gems, but rather for 'its relatively homogenous overall character and its high degree of intactness. The special quality of the area derives from synergism, the whole is greater than the sum of the parts'. Significant recognition of the area was first illustrated by its classification by the National Trust in 1972. This was followed by the completion of a Council commissioned conservation study by Jacobs, Lewis and Vines in 1979; and the publication of *Action Plans Parkville* by the Parkville Community Planning Group (also sponsored by the Council) which had 'widespread involvement and support of Parkville residents' and was adopted as a matter of policy by the Council in July 1980. Ultimately, these initiatives led to the introduction of historic conservation controls by amendment to the planning scheme with a new clause 25L.

• Mr Neesham, QC, for the Wades, argued that since the controls did not *require* restoration, then in the absence of any specific requirement, the intent to *require* should not be read in. The Board concluded that the Council was not *requiring* owners to restore their properties, rather it was witholding its consent to any change 'unless that change would help to preserve, restore or enhance the historical or architectural character of the area'.

• Dr Peter Thorne put the view, and it was so held, that in

relation to the door and window alterations which had already occurred without a permit, '. . . an applicant cannot improve his position by commencing work without a permit'.

• Various arguments were put in relation to the 'relevant starting point'. The residents wished to meet the argument, 'anything is better than the present bomb-site'. The Board held that this was a non-issue since it was not obliged to compare the proposal with any particular yardstick, but that if one were necessary, then the comparison is 'between the proposal, on the one hand, and the probable state of the building if the proposal is rejected'. The Board expressed the view that presumably the building would not remain in its existing state and that a compromise would be reached.

• In the light of the planning controls, the 'fundamental considerations' before the Board were:

(a) Whether the proposed alterations and fence will *conserve* and *enhance* and be in *harmony* with the existing character of South Parkville and, in particular, adjacent buildings.

(b) The effect upon the amenity of the neighbourhood.

• The proposal did not 'conserve and enhance' the historic character of the area because removal of the balcony and wing walls 'radically' changed the appearance of the building. Replacement with 'a flat façade' was a 'critical reason why the proposal would detract from the character of the area'; the windows and doors did not relate to the original design nor to the architecture of the 1880s; the use of mock-historical detailing (e.g. windows and horizontal courses in cement-work) was 'quite harmful as it is liable to confuse the general public as to what is in its original form and what is not'; and the proposed fence, although 'sympathetic', 'contains elements of geometric featurism, such as the recessed gateway and concave top of the gate, which neither conserve nor enhance the historic character of the area'.

• While the inclusion of a balcony 'would undoubtedly involve expense . . . this is essential to conserve and enhance the historic character'. It agreed with the view of Dr Lewis, that if the balcony were restored, then those aspects of the façade design (see above) 'will cease to be conspicuous and could be allowed to remain'.

• These findings were reinforced by the Council's non-statutory, but adopted policy for South Parkville, which was based on the guidelines drawn up by their consultants, Jacobs, Lewis and Vines.

• It was necessary, the Board felt, to respond to Norman Day's '*Burra Charter* defence'. This was carefully disposed of on the basis that, 'completion of the depleted entity would not constitute the majority of the fabric of the "place" (whether "place" was defined as building, area or façade)'. The Board went even further: 'the *Charter* would not have prohibited the "adaption" of the building in order to contribute to the cultural significance of South Parkville'.

In a particularly candid vein, the Board held that Norman Day's reliance on the *Burra Charter* was 'rather belated' and 'lacked credibility'. Much of Day's cross-examination had been less than searching and it fell to Morris, the Chairman, to pursue some aspects and to put him through the hoops. At one stage he examined Day concerning an article he had written in the *Age* about the work of the architect Greg Burgess, and in which Day concluded, 'Burgess has created a schismatic building of public decency and private fantasy; a thoroughly Victorian characteristic. It remains to be seen whether history judges that gesture as sensitive, gentle architectural behaviour or as a lack of confidence'. Morris, it seems, had found the key to Day's ambitions and he therefore came to find:

> It seems to the Board that in designing the Wade house *Mr Day did not want to be accused of having a lack of confidence. Rather Mr Day wanted to stamp his own imprint on South Parkville.* As a general rule this sort of architectural self-confidence is to be applauded . . . But the community, through its government, has designated South Parkville as an area where urban conservation policies should be pursued so that the public could continue to appreciate the work of architects and builders who made their imprint one hundred years ago. This makes Mr Day's design singularly inappropriate, even though it may be quite praiseworthy in another context. (author's italics)

• The proposal would not be in *harmony* with the area, 'primarily because the proposal does not make provision for a balcony or wing walls'. Numbers 11–17 were erected as a set of balcony houses and it was these (and not the single storey house at number 19—cited as a contrasting example by Mr Neesham), 'which establish the character of the streetscape and to which [number 17] primarily relates'. The lack of balcony and wing walls created a *contrast* with these adjoining buildings as well as highlighting differing window and door treatments.

> It is true that *contrast* does not necessarily mean *disharmony*, but this will usually be the case where the beholder expects a group of buildings to match one another . . . This is not to say that each façade must be *identical*, but merely that *each façade must have the same elements*, such as a balcony and wing walls.[4] (author's italics)

For the above reasons, the proposal would also be 'detrimental to the amenity of the neighbourhood'.

• The proposal was accordingly rejected although if it were 'redesigned to include a balcony and wing walls, the proposed alterations could then be seen in a different light' (on the basis that the windows and doors would be less obtrusive).

• A permit for the fence was issued, but strict conditions were attached which required it to be in accordance with the fence at number 15.

• An appeal by Dr and Mrs Ken Brown regarding a trellis fence at the rear of the Wade property did not 'involve conservation issues', and was disallowed on the basis that its height of 2.44 metres, considering its set-back from the side boundaries, would not seriously affect the overshadowing of the Browns' property. The actual loss of sunlight to the Browns' rear garden was estimated at 1.2 metres on 21 June each year and the Board regarded this as 'somewhat trivial'.

• In a dissenting opinion, Rita Avdiev made a plea for freedom of architectural expression. 'Post-modernism/contextualism is not yet a strong force. Until there are enough examples of this style in Australia, the public eye will not become accustomed to it.' She reminded us of the resistance encountered by innovators such as Leonardo Da Vinci and the French Impressionists and said that the controls did not provide 'specific instructions as to design details and features . . . [nor] lead one to the conclusion that it is important or necessary to retain the wing walls or balcony of No. 17 Fitzgibbon Street . . .'

The Board incisively threaded its way through the subtle complexities of the conservation issues. Only two or three years previously Phil Opas, QC, had refused to concede that the word 'streetscape' had any legitimate place in the Board's vocabulary. The Board was now, with the advent of conservation controls, regarding it as an essential term in determining the character of the neighbourhood. Problems normally encountered with terms like *conservation*, *enhancement*, *contrast*, *subjectivity*, and even the *Burra Charter* and *anastylosis* were all dealt with quickly and effectively.

One further matter is worth noting. The solicitor for the Council, Ian Murray, recently made the comment to me that the Wades were unlucky in that the conservation controls were imposed about a year before the hearing. It seems highly likely that the publicity given to the Wade house case acted as a catalyst for the introduction of the urban conservation area controls. In fact, however, the Board held that the Council's adopted policies were still relevant in this case as were sound town planning principles generally, regardless of the introduction of the new controls via the amending clause 25L. It held that the 'proposal and fence would be detrimental to the amenity of the neighbourhood' and it could well have rejected them solely on that basis alone. We will of course, never know what the Board would have done prior to the existence of urban conservation area controls, but the opportunity to reject the Wade proposals was certainly there in the light of the extensive history of Council planning policies for the area.[5]

Time and Money

The hearing was disposed of in only four days despite the complexity of many of the issues. Residents, who represented themselves, were not faced with any legal or expert evidence fees and there are no court fees applicable to such hearings. The Council did not engage a barrister so that it only incurred the fees of its solicitor Ian Murray, and those of its expert witnesses such as Miles Lewis and Darren Overend. The National Trust's witnesses and barrister, Craig Porter, were entirely honorary and its solicitor, Julia Bruce of Russell, Kennedy & Cook, appeared on a reduced fee basis. The Wades were involved in much more expense (estimated at $27,000) since they chose to engage a Queen's Counsel, junior barrister, solicitor and expert witnesses (valuer, planner and architect). While this was unfortunate for them it was the result of an investment decision made *by them*, presumably based upon professional advice. It was *their* decision to appeal and oppose the Council, its independent consultants, the Parkville objectors and the National Trust.

Although bold and clever, Norman Day's proposal was deemed by the Board to fly in the face of the endorsed conservation principles of the South Parkville conservation area. Day still believes it should have been approved. It was defeated by a combination of local opposition, sound expert evidence, and more particularly by a Board endowed with intellectual capacity, an understanding of conservation and planning issues, and a shrewd ability to make personal assessments.

Footnotes
1 Actual words deleted due to defamation laws.
2 The *Age*, 26 June 1982.
3 Determination of the Appeals Board, p. 25.
4 *Ibid*, p. 28.
5 *City of Fitzroy v. Australian Aluminium Shopfitters & Glazing Contractors Pty Ltd*, Planning Appeals Board, P82/1162, is an example of a case where the Board rejected a permit on historical and aesthetic grounds without specific statutory provisions.

3

The Rear of The House and the Breakdown of Reason

> It is not unfair to observe that the Town Clerk and other Council officers adopted an unbending attitude towards the residents and were singularly unsympathetic to their proposals.
>
> *Justice O'Bryan*[1]

Justice O'Bryan also commented that the residents embarked upon a 'remarkable crusade'. If to 'crusade' is to diligently defend one's neighbourhood from unlawful developments which will adversely affect the area, then hopefully, civic minded citizens should be encouraged to crusade within the spirit of our town planning law.

Let us then consider the position that confronted the residents. When they discovered from Norman Day's plans that there was to be a rear extension to the Wade house they immediately sought information. Enquiries at the Town Hall elicited various responses: that the extensions were only single storey; that they did not extend beyond the existing walls; and that the Wades were spending 'a lot of money on it'. The plans were singularly unhelpful since without elevations or other dimensional plans it was impossible to appreciate the scale and potential impact of the building.[2]

Letters were sent to the Town Clerk seeking particulars concerning the scale, height, plot ratio and extent of overshadowing. Some letters were ignored while others received tardy and confusing replies. Once the magnitude of the structure was appreciated—that is, an addition extending right across the block to the boundaries on both sides, measuring 7.2 metres long and approximately 10.5 metres high—the residents knew beyond doubt that a major mistake had been made.

For people who do not live in the highly populated inner suburbs, something should be said about the fragile relationship between buildings, sunlight and gardens. Rear gardens normally provide the only recreational areas of terrace houses in the inner suburbs. The houses sit cheek by jowl—hemmed in on either side. Generally, the only opportunity for privacy, quiet and outdoor space is at the rear.

In the present case, Day argued that in the inner suburbs you cannot expect privacy and freedom from overlooking. I do not believe this view is acceptable to competent town planners in Victoria.

The impact of the Wade development was widely canvassed but one of the best assessments was never allowed to be seen by the court. Lawrie Wilson, the independent consultant briefed by the Council in July 1982, fairly accurately predicted the judge's findings when he reported:

> . . . two storey buildings normally extend to a similar depth at the upper level where it is common to locate a bedroom . . . the extension went well beyond the rear of the existing structure . . . and by extending across the full width of the site was totally inconsistent historically, with terrace house design . . . [It was] . . . therefore unduly intrusive to the surrounding properties to a degree which may be unacceptable and potentially detrimental to the amenity of the surrounding area.

Wilson was particularly critical of the potential for overlooking which was, 'far greater than would normally occur'. He concluded that the extensions might cause substantial detriment and in words that the judge himself almost chose, commented: 'I acknowledge that the adjoining owners had given their consent to the proposed development, however I do not accept that this indicates that the adjoining owners are prepared to accept the detriment which may potentially result . . .'

Wilson advised the Council that it should have formed the opinion that the extensions may cause substantial detriment, that the proposal should have been advertised and that the failure to so act meant a breach of section 18B of the Planning Act. He did not say what everyone knew; that such a breach meant that the permit was invalid and the building illegal.

It seemed incredible that such an extension could be permitted. In most Melbourne suburbs buildings are altogether prohibited on side boundaries. In areas like South Parkville, control is normally exercised through the application of plot ratio (that is, the ratio between floor cover to total site). It seemed clear that the new building involved a considerable increase in floor cover as well as height. The solicitor for the residents calculated that the floor cover would be increased from 300.39 square metres to 316.8 square metres. However, in its defence, the Council followed their practice of including a number of shanty structures to the rear of the property which had been built without permits. By including these illegal, now demolished structures (three aviaries, a laundry and a garage), they said that the proposed floor cover would in fact be slightly reduced or about the same.

While the residents were anxiously trying to find out what was going on, demolition commenced with workmen knocking down Notini's side brick wall. It was at this point that the Thornes and others knew that there was a *real* problem and that they were either going to turn their backs on their helpless neighbours or get involved. The reader will have his own view as to what action should have been taken, but even today, years after all the anguish and crippling financial and other problems, the residents are adamant that there was no other alternative possible and that they would make the same decision again if the circumstances were repeated.

Considerable difficulties were encountered in trying to get anyone in authority to co-operate and explain what had happened. Neither Thorley, the Chief Commissioner, nor Bethke, the Town Clerk, would even meet with the residents although Bethke was quite happy to talk to Wade and his advisers on various occasions—even to the extent of opening up the Town Hall offices for a Saturday morning meeting.

The residents knew that something had gone wrong but the problem was to identify precisely what, how and why. In a letter sent to the City Solicitor on 24 June 1983, Blake & Riggall requested answers to twenty-four questions. They sought information concerning the nature of the extensions, the calculations relating to floor cover, the basis for Council denying the existence of a party wall between the Wades' and the Notinis' properties, details of any perceived impact caused by overshadowing, site inspections, transcript of the revocation proceedings, the basis for Council's belief that it had complied with s. 18B of the Planning Act, copies of correspondence with the Ombudsman, etc. A Council acting responsibly would have known it had nothing to hide and would have responded to almost all the questions which for the most part sought only basic factual information that should have been freely available. The Council did not respond to the questions.

Clearly, however, an error had been made and as Justice O'Bryan was to find, the proposed development was a 'disaster', at least for the Browns to the south. The residents maintained that no neighbour in his right mind would have voluntarily agreed to such a development. Miss Chisholm and Notini were adamant that when signing their 'consent' on the plan shown them by Doug Wade, they had had no idea of the actual size and impact of the development and that at no stage did anyone disclose what was really proposed. In fact, elevation plans and a three-dimensional model had been prepared by Day but these were never shown to them. Notini and Chisholm maintained that Wade misrepresented the proposal to them. At this point, however, they felt too apprehensive to become actively involved and were content to rely upon their neighbours to pursue the problem for them.

The residents kept asking—what went wrong? Had the Council officers been tricked, did they understand the true nature of the proposal, or were they just plain sloppy in their handling of the application? Dealing with the Council was unbelievably frustrating. Correspondence was frequently ignored or only partly answered. The bureaucracy closed ranks. In an effort to obtain information the residents referred the matter to the State Ombudsman who managed to obtain a summary response from the Town Clerk. In this, Bethke described the development as an 'application, which involved, *inter alia*, substantial internal alterations and the addition of a deck at first floor . . .'[3] There was no reference to the *real* problem, namely the substantial rear extensions running right across the block to the neighbours' boundaries. Perhaps, the residents told themselves, the Council officers were even now still unaware of the real nature of the problem. One may judge from the plan submitted and reproduced on page 44 whether it is possible to obtain an adequate appreciation of the impact of the development upon surrounding properties.

It was also apparent that officers were confused as to their responsibilities. The Town Clerk had stated that in relation to the issue of notifying residents of the application, the Acting City Planner, John Noonan, had given consideration to whether any other person was likely to be 'aggrieved'. However, the requirement under the Act was whether any person might suffer 'substantial detriment'. In practice, the distinction is important, since many people may feel subjectively aggrieved, but this does not mean that they will suffer substantial detriment, as was pointed out by Wilson.

It was thus difficult to feel confident that Council officers really understood what was involved, what impact the extension would have and whether, on balance, a reasonable assessment had been made of its acceptability. Many Councillors believed the correspondence from Bethke was inadequate and certainly it was defensive. For example, he said he resented the allegation that the matter had been 'rushed through' and claimed that it had been very carefully considered indeed. In fact, it was revealed that the application had lain dormant on Miss Lucy Lieuw's desk for nearly three weeks, until two days before Christmas when pressure was applied for it to be processed.

In frustration, the residents had written to the Ombudsman and to their solicitors who wrote to the Town Clerk. Bethke's next move was to refer all further correspondence to the City Solicitor, Ian Murray, who pulled the hatches down firmly. He advised the Ombudsman that, 'In my opinion there is no substance whatever in any of the complaints made', and given the commencement of legal proceedings, suggested that the Ombudsman, 'should refuse to conduct any investigations'.[4]

The following story will serve to illustrate the kinds of frustrations visited upon the residents. They had heard on the grapevine that Norman Day had made a three-dimensional model of the house complete with extensions and that he had placed it on the table at a meeting at the Town Hall, in front of Wade, Council advisers and officers including Bethke and Noonan.

Blake & Riggall sought to obtain information about the model, thinking it might be of use at the Supreme Court hearing to illustrate graphically what was proposed. Ian Murray replied to the solicitors that despite careful enquiries, no one had any recollection of any such model! The mystery was not solved until the Supreme Court hearing when Neil Brown (for the residents) casually asked Wade, in cross-examination, what had happened to the model. He replied that he had possession of it and then revealed that it was safely stored in the boot of his car! Later that day the judge ordered that it be brought to court and it finally saw the light of day after being in the car for some months.

Overall, this lack of co-operation meant that the residents were forced to make several alternative claims. They did not know how the building application had been assessed by the Council and there seemed no way of finding out. They therefore based their assertions on the information available and claimed that the assessment was inadequate, that the wrong criterion had been adopted (when deciding whether to notify neighbours), and that there had been misrepresentation. This is standard legal practice, the assumption being that you normally only have to win on one leg to establish the case (that is, invalidity of the permit).

It is true that in the early stages, the residents were adamant that misrepresentation should also be vigorously pursued. They maintained firmly that Notini and Chisholm had been tricked by Wade and that Day was quilty of deception. At the injunction hearing before Justice Gobbo, the residents' counsel, Peter Hayes, emphasized that this was a major component of the case. However, by the time the case itself came on before the Supreme Court, counsel had wisely relegated the issue to one of much lesser significance.

The earlier course of action proved to be the residents' one major error. They were filled with a sense of righteous indignation against Wade and Day. They saw Wade as a man who crashed through, oblivious to the concerns of the innocent, elderly and weak who stood in his way. Convinced of his fault, they were adamant from the start that he should be exposed for what they saw as deliberate misrepresentation. They were incensed by what they regarded as his maltreatment of the elderly Chisholm and the shy immigrant Notini.

Wade had been told by Day that his application would be processed quickly if he could obtain the consent of his neighbours. He therefore went and saw Notini and Chisholm separately with plans which they signed consenting to the proposal. He maintained in evidence that he explained everything to them in detail and that nothing was witheld. They, on the contrary, maintained that he had said nothing of the rear extensions, that the plans did not adequately indicate there and that he had refrained from showing them the elevations or model which would have clearly illustrated what was proposed. Miss Chisholm swore that, 'I consider it would have been a simple matter for Mr Wade to have explained to me what he had proposed for the rear of his house', and stated that if she had known of the rear extensions reaching right across to her boundary, she would have objected to the application.

As we shall see, the allegations were counter-productive and most damaging to the residents' cause. To allege but not prove misrepresentation had direct consequences in relation to costs and may very well have influenced the judge when he came to exercise his discretion. In February of the following year Miss Chisholm died and there was discussion as to whether there would be sufficient evidence to succeed on the issue. Greg Garde, barrister for the residents, advocated withdrawing it and subsequently recommended that a court order be sought to determine the admissability of the affidavits obtained from Miss Chisholm prior to her death. The advice unfortunately was not accepted since Alex Chernov, QC, who was the residents' senior barrister at that stage, directed that the matter be left in abeyance until the hearing. A costly decision as it transpired.

Miss Chisholm was almost on her deathbed in St Vincent's Hospital when she signed her second affidavit. With tears in her eyes, she charged solicitors Simon Molesworth and Rod Bush to 'tell them what really happened on that night'. The two solicitors were visiting Miss Chisholm to take the affidavit with Gavin Forrest, Commissioner for taking affidavits, her doctor, nephew and nursing sister. They saw a woman withered and shrunken with cancer but who was resolute. To hear the force of her words and her powerful desire to have them recorded proved a harrowing experience. Her affidavit records:

> Mr Wade states that I 'had no objection whatsoever to the plans and signed them quite willingly'. I consider it is essential that I stress that Mr Wade's account is wrong. Contrary to being willing to sign the plans I was very unsure as to whether I should do so. Accordingly I hesitated which resulted in Mr Wade repeating at three separate intervals with increasing emphasis a demand that I should sign. I deliberately used the word 'demand' as on the last occasion he forcibly banged the plans with his fingers, loudly directing me to sign it. In the cirumstances I signed it.[5]

The conversation was heard (through the kitchen doorway) by her border, Sydney Fahey, who was having a cup of tea in the adjacent room. He explained later that he told Miss Chisholm that she had done the wrong thing in signing the plans. When he was subsequently approached by Molesworth, he proved to be extraordinarily reticent and a frightened, introverted character who refused to help by giving evidence.

Miss Chisholm died just three days after signing her second affidavit. The position was reviewed and counsel for the residents put it to me that he explained to the residents the difficulty of proving misrepresentation, that it was a serious charge and that costs could be awarded against them if they lost. The residents do not recall any such conversation but I have no doubt that as laymen, and given the complexity of the case, they simply failed to fully absorb the significance of the matter. They also felt a deep sense of loyalty to Miss Chisholm and that therefore, the claim should not be dropped since it would be dishonourable to her memory. Honour at a price! The issue proved the Achilles heel for the residents. They made little headway against Day with the various plans and the death of Chisholm removed a prime witness. The case against Wade boiled down to his word against that of the diffident, halting Notini. Wade was to win in a canter.

The misrepresentation issue was cleverly and thoroughly emphasized by Tom Neesham, counsel for the Wades. He constantly attacked the residents as a hostile 'rabble' who were uncompromising to the Wades and he was wholly successful in his strategy.

I should like to emphasize that I am not here seeking to place Wade and Day on trial for things which were extensively canvassed before the Supreme Court. They were both exonerated completely and the court record is plainly there for all to see. I can make no comment as to such matters. The truth is, I simply don't know anyway. My purpose has simply been to try and get inside the minds of the residents, to explain how they felt and why they did what they did. Whether they were foolish, justified or ill-advised must ultimately be for the reader to decide.

To Court . . . To Court . . .

The Wades did not wish to negotiate further. They had slightly amended their plans by deleting the sun-deck from the first floor of the building, which reduced the extent of overlooking. However, this did almost nothing to reduce the overall bulk of the extensions. The residents had to decide whether to give up and allow the development to proceed, or to pursue what they perceived as their democratic rights in town planning law. Their problems were compounded due to the fact that they did not always agree on all issues. Moreover, their case was weakened by the attitude of Notini and Miss Chisholm, who at this stage were still not parties to the action. The residents had asked what they could do to solve the problem without litigation. Virtually everyone they spoke to, from government advisers to lawyers, agreed that a dreadful mistake had occurred. As Dr Michael Henry, a senior ministerial adviser to Evan Walker said, 'Some cases just have to go to court'.

It was also fair to say that widespread support for the residents came from many quarters. Many of the now dismissed Councillors were outraged by what had occurred. Bill Gardiner, shortly to be elected Lord Mayor, recalls standing on a ladder supported by ex-Councillor Richard Malone. He was peering over the fence from the Notinis' property, endeavouring to take a photograph of the work in progress, to be greeted by a workman who threatened to hose him down! Nothing daunted, he encouraged the residents to fight on.

The residents were also encouraged to 'hang in there' in the hope that the Council might revoke the permit under section 24 of the Act, although this would be unprecedented. After examining the residents' affidavits, the Commissioners resolved to commence proceedings for the permit to 'be revoked on the ground of material mis-statement or conceal-

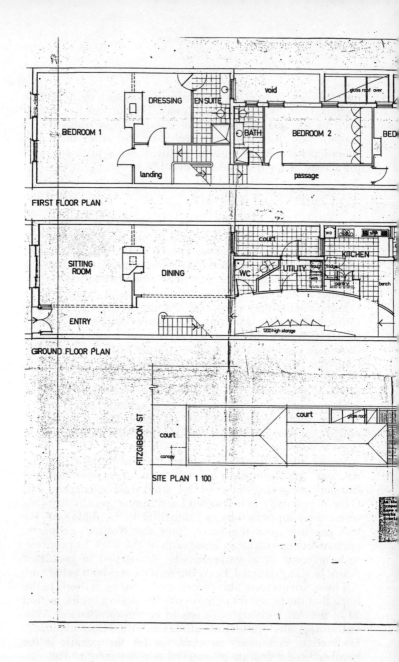

FIRST FLOOR PLAN

BEDROOM 1
DRESSING
EN SUITE
void
glass roof over
BATH
BEDROOM 2
BED
landing
passage

GROUND FLOOR PLAN

SITTING ROOM
DINING
court
wo
KITCHEN
WC
UTILITY
fridge
pantry
bench
ENTRY
1200 high storage

SITE PLAN 1 100

FITZGIBBON ST
court
canopy
court
glass roof

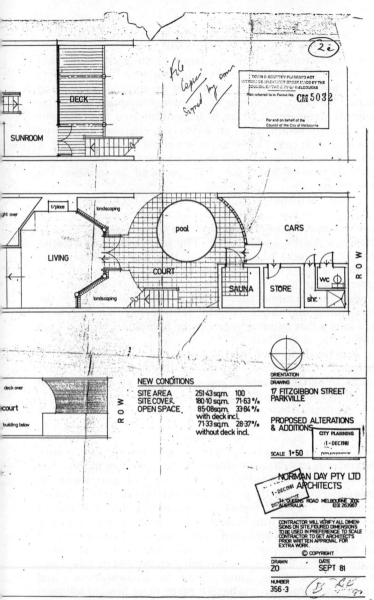

Within the plan:

DECK

SUNROOM

t/place   landscaping

pool

CARS

R O W

LIVING

COURT

SAUNA   STORE   wc

shr.

deck over

court

building below

R O W

ORIENTATION

DRAWING

17 FITZGIBBON STREET
PARKVILLE

NEW CONDITIONS

SITE AREA   251·43 sqm.   100
SITE COVER   180·10 sqm.   71·63 %
OPEN SPACE   85·08 sqm.   33·84 %
               with deck incl.
               71·33 sqm.   28·37%
               without deck incl.

PROPOSED ALTERATIONS
& ADDITIONS

CITY PLANNING
·1 - DEC 1981

SCALE 1" 50

TOWN & COUNTRY PLANNING ACT
INTERIM DEVELOPMENT ORDER MADE BY THE
COUNCIL OF THE CITY OF MELBOURNE
Plan referred to in Permit No. CM 5032

For and on behalf of the
Council of the City of Melbourne

NORMAN DAY PTY LTD
ARCHITECTS
1 - DEC 1981
24 QUEENS ROAD MELBOURNE 3XX
AUSTRALIA   (03) 263967

CONTRACTOR WILL VERIFY ALL DIMEN-
SIONS ON SITE. FIGURED DIMENSIONS
TO BE USED IN PREFERENCE TO SCALE
CONTRACTOR TO GET ARCHITECT'S
PRIOR WRITTEN APPROVAL FOR
EXTRA WORK.
© COPYRIGHT

DRAWN   DATE
ZO   SEPT 81

NUMBER
356·3

The 'collage' plans (at least three plans pasted together), signed by
Miss Chisholm indicating her 'consent'. Courtesy Norman Day.

45

ment of fact made in or in relation to the grant of the said permit'.[6] The Chairman of Commissioners, Peter Thorley, made the announcement public and proceedings were set in train. However, in the light of the construction work now rapidly proceeding, Blake & Riggall advised the residents that their position could be severely prejudiced if building continued. It could serve to pre-empt the issue of whether it should be built at all and the Wades could show loss and damage consequent upon any proposal to remove the extension.

It has been subsequently claimed by Alex Chernov, QC, that the residents were 'aware for some months . . . that construction was in progress and that accordingly they should have acted with greater speed'. This is a very complex matter but it is critical since it is clear that if the residents had managed to get the case into court sooner, and assuming the permit were held invalid, they would have won and thus ended the litigation and spiralling legal costs. Perhaps the first thing that might be said, however, is that Chernov's claim is rather extravagant since the foundations had still not been poured by 7 July.

The residents and their advisers put their position in a number of ways. First, they viewed litigation as a last resort, to be undertaken only if and when negotiations had failed irretrievably. Second, the main issue concerned the validity of the permit based on s. 18B and since no one had ever succeeded in a challenge on this issue before, there was inevitably some concern to proceed cautiously. Third, the solicitors for the Wades had given verbal assurances that work would not extend into the disputed areas, pending the outcome of negotiations. Fourth, the Council had announced its intention to revoke the permit at a special hearing on 12 August which invited the prospect of imminent resolution at no cost to the residents. Fifth, Murray, who was obviously a very key figure, had intimated that the residents were likely to succeed in the revocation proceedings, and he expressed strong reservations about the Council becoming embroiled in a Supreme Court action which could offend the Commissioners and therefore be counter-productive. Sixth, three firms of solicitors for the residents wrote to the Wades' solicitors prior to construction commencing. They warned them that it was proposed to pursue the matter before the Supreme Court if necessary and that if work continued in the face of negotiations, it would be put that such refusal to cease work would be led in evidence against the Wades.

Blake & Riggall suggested various proposals in an effort to resolve the dispute, all of which sought to ensure that the Wades would apply for a valid permit which would be subject to the normal public review process. The firm had adhered to their instructions to avoid litigation wherever possible, but it was now obviously necessary to act promptly to prevent the residents' position being prejudiced by further building. On 12 and 19 July, Blake & Riggall were compelled to write to the Wades' solicitors pointing out that:

> Despite assurances work has continued—the workmen on site are now working for significant periods after hours including throughout the last weekend. Our clients have made every effort to avoid causing cost . . . Given the inevitable cost and delays associated with Supreme Court proceedings and given the consideration that our respective clients will be obliged to live as neighbours irrespective of the outcome of the present issues, we believe that every effort should be made to resolve this issue as equitably and as expeditiously as possible. However, we must confirm that we have explicit instructions to proceed to the Supreme Court forthwith unless a satisfactory resolution is achieved.

Large scale photographs which are exhibits to sworn affidavits on the court file clearly illustrate the state of the works at the time. On 7 July workmen were excavating for foundations. Brickwork on the walls of the building still continued almost until the summons was issued on 30 July, and at the time of the hearing before Justice Gobbo on 3 August, work to the disputed upstairs sunroom area consisted only of two very raw brick walls 10–12 feet high and to the west, a mere lintel and pediment suspended above fresh air. There was no roofing, flooring, internal or external finishes or services of any kind. The cost of this work has been estimated at $5000–$5700 by a quantity surveyor. It was obviously only a modest part of the total work to be done but, all the same, it was no mean achievement for three weeks work. In point of fact only eight clear working days elapsed between the date of commencement of work on the disputed upper storey and the 30 July (issue of the writ and summons for an injunction).

Given this background, should the residents have jumped into court sooner and sought an injunction? Opinion is divided. Even with hindsight, it is extremely difficult to make such judgements. However, my own views are as follows: first, I believe that in all the complex circumstances, the residents and their advisers moved with reasonable speed consistent with the need to keep negotiating options open. Secondly, I now suspect that they were a little naïve and may have been lulled into a false sense of security by the assurances given both by the Council's and the Wades' solicitors concerning prospects for a negotiated settlement. In view of the Wades' propensity for rapid construction, perhaps the residents should have realised sooner that negotiations were unlikely to yield success and that the Wades would do their utmost to pre-empt the due processes by continuing to build. Given their keen desire to seek a negotiated settlement, it is not clear whether they could have got into court sufficiently early to have ultimately changed the outcome — bearing in mind the attitude adopted by Justice Gobbo.[7]

The Injunction Hearing

> If the residents succeed in the end they suffer no greater hardship . . .
>
> *Justice Gobbo*[8]

The Wades had declined to negotiate further, declined to apply for a permit subject to the normal review processes and by pressing ahead with construction, placed the residents in the position of having to put up, shut up, or litigate. The residents had reluctantly issued a writ and applied for an injunction to prevent further construction prior to the main hearing itself. The injunction hearing came on before Justice Gobbo in the Practice Court on 3 August 1982.

In a decision which was to have the most serious consequences for the residents, Justice Gobbo declined to hear the application. It is beyond argument that if the whole case had come on for trial at that time (and the permit found to be invalid then), the Wades would have been sent back to apply for a fresh permit and the residents would have succeeded. The inability of the residents to obtain an injunction enabled rapid completion of the building and this was ultimately the decisive factor which later dissuaded Justice O'Bryan from requiring demolition when he exercised his discretion.

Peter Hayes, the barrister for the residents, stated at the outset that an injunction was sought to 'hold the status quo'.[9] He said that the 'works were proceeding [pursuant to an] . . . invalid permit . . . [which had been] . . . misleadingly obtained'.[10]

Hayes went on to argue that the effect of continuing construction would be to prejudice the residents since ultimately, when the case itself was litigated, the judge would have to exercise his discretion, and weigh up 'factors on [the] balance of convenience'[11] and therefore, the court would be faced with a *fait accompli*. It was also explained that the Council had announced its intention to revoke the permit and to convene a hearing to consider revocation on 12 August.

Justice Gobbo was advised of the allegations of misrepresentation and he quickly expressed concern that an injunction hearing might largely duplicate the issues at the main trial itself and that in any event, an injunction might be obviated by the Council revocation hearing.

Justice Gobbo firmly countered the claim that the residents would be prejudiced by any further construction, by saying, 'if the residents succeed in the end they suffer no greater hardship and the hardship that has been suffered in the interim will be taken into account by the Court'.[12] The judge then indicated that the residents would not be prejudiced since it was not necessary to preserve the status quo, citing the precedent of the Pasley Street South Yarra case where a developer had continued construction in the face of a legal challenge to the permit and was ultimately required to demolish a completed block of flats. Tom Neesham, on behalf of the Wades, supported the judge's approach stating that the residents' position would not be eroded since:

> This court can order they be undone . . . if the building was found to be in breach of the permit, it would have to come down. No damage would be sustained by the residents, other than to look for a longer time at works they said were offensive . . .'.[13]

The hearing adjourned at 12.15 and during the break, Peter Hayes advised the residents privately that clearly the judge's mind was made up and accordingly there was nothing to be gained by further pressing for an injunction. He put it to them squarely that the Practice Court was not designed for protracted hearings and that the judge had to resolve a solution to the problem on the balance of conveniences and on the basis that the status quo was preserved. Obviously, he said, it would be inconvenient to halt all construction and there were real difficulties in hearing the summons for an injunction because of the volume of evidentiary material. On the other hand, he said, the judge had explained that it would be more convenient to get the summons listed quickly in the normal causes list and that in the meantime, the residents position would not be eroded by delays and further construction. I was present for this meeting and indeed, for the duration of the hearing.

The judge returned to advise that enquiries had revealed a prospect of the Summons for the Injunction being heard on 9 September, and concluded that, 'I am not persuaded to request the Court to hear an application today for an injunction under the Practice Court procedures'[14] due to the time involved in such a hearing and because the residents will not be adversely affected as a consequence. His parting comment to the Wades when he turned to them on his left was that the 'residents [are] concerned that [their] task [is] harder if building proceeds. *Any step the defendants take from this point on they take at their peril*'[15] and '. . . if in the end the residents succeed, the residents will have their remedies'.[16] (author's italics)

It has subsequently been claimed by Alex Chernov that the residents did not press for an injunction. I can only respond by saying that the above account is consistent with all the documentation to which I have obtained access and, more importantly, accords with my own personal recollection. Chernov's involvement was initiated by Justice Gobbo and the former concluded that it was a consent order of the parties, which clearly, it was not.

Certainly, the residents went in to bat for an injunction — why else were they there? As Tom Neesham, for the Wades commented, '. . . it did not succeed . . . before His Honour it was taken that any application for an injunction was going to be resisted, and no order for an injunction was made, but precisely why not is a matter that I would not wish now to be bound by . . .'[17]

The judge then went on to make the order for a 'hearing at the earliest possible date in September 1982 subject to the directions of the Listing Master'. At the same time, at the request of the residents, leave was granted to join Notini and Chisholm as additional parties to the action. Regrettably, no record (other than the formal order) of the proceedings in the Practice Court was kept. This gave rise to some difficulties, as we shall see. Nevertheless, reconstruction of the significant statements has been straightforward since there were many people present who took notes and prepared written reports which I have found to be remarkably consistent with my own personal recollection and notes.[18]

Although the residents were disappointed with the result, they were fortified by Justice Gobbo's assurances and by his specific warning to the Wades in the context of the precedent of the demolition of the Pasley Street, South Yarra, flats. The judge had made it very clear to the Wades that they were inviting danger if they thought they could advance their position through building in defiance of the due legal processes. The purpose of the hearing had been to prevent the residents' position being prejudiced and the judge was well satisfied that there was no danger of this occurring since, 'He said he should hear the application now only if he were satisfied that it was imperative to preserve the status quo'.[19] Alas, this assumption was ultimately proved wrong.

The Wades pressed on with their building and with further litigation. They went back to the Supreme Court seeking an Order against the Council for a Declaration preventing it from initiating the revocation of permit proceedings. They argued that the Council's resolution to revoke the permit disclosed that it had wrongly pre-judged the matter. Once again they came before Justice Gobbo and this time, on 6 August 1982, the judge found against the Wades stating they would be given a proper opportunity to be heard.

And so the Melbourne City Council convened its first revocation hearing. It was to be another first for the saga and for the Council. Certainly it was to continue the extraordinary inability of the principal players to reasonably resolve the

51

dispute. What should have been disposed of at an early stage was gradually becoming a nightmare and nobody, save the lawyers, was to be spared.

Revocation of Permit Hearing

The hearing by the Commissioners for revocation of the permit took place at the Town Hall on Thursday 12 August 1982. The three Commissioners were Messrs Thorley, Smith and Alston. The hearing took place in camera in accordance with the Town and Country Planning Act Regulations. Those present included only the Commissioners, the Town Clerk, the Acting City Planner John Noonan, the City Solicitor Ian Murray, Doug and Raelene Wade, Norman Day, and Bill Carroll, solicitor for the Wades. The Regulations gave no right of access to the residents to enable them to be present.

It is not clear how, given such procedures, the legislation might contemplate that justice might be done, let alone, be seen to be done. Affidavits from the residents, two letters and an affidavit from their solicitors, represented the only material which could be considered on behalf of the aggrieved residents and not for the first time, they were denied participation. The unsworn affidavit of Mrs Marina Notini was not considered, although the Wades and the others present were permitted to put, 'whatever you wish to place before the Council . . .' and their unsworn evidence was readily accepted. The attitudes of the Wades, Norman Day and their solicitor Bill Carroll were predictable. Some residents and councillors have held the view that Ian Murray was consistently unsympathetic to the residents because inevitably, he was required to defend the position of the Council. In fairness, he has on several occasions exerted himself in an effort to achieve a settlement and he certainly performed conscientiously against the Wades on behalf of the Council at the Appeals Board hearing regarding the front of the house. Mr Bethke's sympathies soon became apparent (he was later adjudged in the Supreme Court to have been 'singularly unsympathetic'), while John Noonan was placed in the invidious position of having to defend his decision to grant the permit.

In such circumstances, it is difficult to take the consequent proceedings seriously. The residents were not permitted to respond to any of the arguments put favouring the Wades nor to counter criticisms made against them. Blake & Riggall had sought an opportunity to comment further and Thorley had said at the outset that this was 'a matter for our discretion'. However, the Wades' solicitor argued against any such opportunity and Murray supported him, saying he was 'totally in agreement with what Mr Carroll says . . . My advice would be that we do not countenance any further material from the objectors . . .'[20]

Thus it was impossible to counter absurd statements from Mr Carroll, for example: 'So far as the question of amenity is concerned, it is considered that completion of the dwelling house as planned and approved will enhance the amenity . . . As to the question of overlooking and overshadowing, these are "occupational hazards" for any resident living in a closer or inner suburban area . . .'[21] And so it went on. At various stages aspersions were cast upon the residents and their motives while Mr and Mrs Wade were lauded as 'people of integrity and honesty and this is well recognised by the public at large'.

The Commissioners were obviously puzzled and found it difficult to understand the real nature of the problem. Both Wade and his solicitor earnestly stated that it was their intention to restore the building to the Victorian period! An extract from the transcript will provide an example of the Commissioners at their busy best:

MR ALSTON: If a number of other properties have been done up in this manner, why are the residents jumping up and down as a body?

MR CARROLL: It remains a mystery.

MR WADE: We wish we knew that. We have a feeling why.

MRS WADE: They wanted the publicity.

MR WADE: That is one of the things; their group wanted publicity, and unfortunately for us they found they could get it.

MR ALSTON: What do they want you to do—leave the whole place alone?

MR DAY: I think there is a movement to have their action plan made law at the council level. I think this is an issue about which they can get publicity for that plan, and that is what they are doing, and as a lead-up to the election it is pretty good politics.

This ridiculous dialogue was followed by a . . . '(Short discussion off the record)'.

The Commissioners were in the awkward position of having conflicting material before them. On the one hand they had sworn affidavits by the residents alleging misrepresentation while on the other they found themselves in the presence of a group of participants who clearly had no sympathy for the residents. This inevitably prevented any rigorous and fair testing of the assertions. How were they to deal with this conflicting written material? Commissioner Smith found a solution:

MR SMITH: Mr Wade has sworn in his Affidavit, and it is rather irrelevant for me to comment on what you have already sworn, but I would like to look you in the face, and you do likewise to me, and to ask you: you have sworn that no material mis-statement or concealment of fact had been made to either Miss Chisholm or Mr Notini . . .
MR WADE: None at all—certainly not at all. As I said, the only thing I did say was about the pool at the back . . . and I went into complete detail [about the two storeyed extensions at the rear] . . .

How on earth it could be contemplated that such a hearing pursuant to the Regulations might provide any form of real justice remains a mystery. The Wades' solicitor repeated his earlier request that the residents be prevented from responding to the submissions and allegations made. Murray again supported the Wades' position and Thorley thereupon changed his mind, agreed with Murray and the hearing concluded forthwith.

The Commissioners accordingly had no difficulty deciding at their meeting on 18 August 1982, that 'there had not been any material mis-statement or concealment of fact made in or in relation to the application for the permit, it accordingly hereby resolves that it will not submit to the said Minister any recommendation in writing in relation to this matter'.

As Carroll had observed, the onus of proof placed upon

the residents was 'a burdensome one' and how they could be expected to discharge it *in absentia* is beyond comprehension. Admittedly, following this affair, the revocation provisions were amended but considerable difficulties remain today—not the least of which is that there is still no requirement that aggrieved persons may have an opportunity to be present.

Further, the principal defects remain, in that aggrieved persons cannot initiate proceedings, must rely on the goodwill of those who have an interest in denying they are in error and thereafter, whether there is a hearing or not, there is no opportunity for them to appeal to the Appeals Board—save for the holder of the so-called permit (the alleged 'guilty' party). It should be added that not only do Councils have obvious political motives for denying error, they will also naturally be wary of making any admissions which might lead to litigation for negligence.

Indeed, it is understood that the sole reason why the proceedings did not focus upon a mistake of fact or law, rather than misrepresentation, was that the Council was concerned at the potential for a negligence action against it. Thus the Council could not make the finding that the Supreme Court eventually made because of its fear of litigation—an obviously absurd situation. Clearly, too, it is much easier to prove a mistake of fact or law, which were the other grounds, than a material mis-statement or concealment of fact.

A further point is of interest. It was not the first time that Norman Day had made allegations to the effect that the residents had political motives—presumably to seek conservation controls for the area. It is possible that he persuaded the Wades to genuinely believe this. The charge is ridiculous. None of the residents had had any experience whatever of resident action or conservation planning. None of them knew anything of 'revocation', 'section 18B', 'planning ordinances' or anything else of consequence to do with town planning. Moreover, at this stage, their principal concern was the rear of the house—the issues that Mr Carroll had advanced in his submissions at the hearing concerning the front and historic conservation controls were a complete red herring.

The 'Thirty-eight Steps'

As Justice Gobbo had ordered that the case be heard 'at the earliest possible date', the residents confidently looked forward to it coming on quickly. Alas, this was not to be.

Two of the Callovers held by the Listing Master in August were cancelled but Simon Molesworth obtained a hearing date before Justice Lush on 11 October for hearing the summons for the injunction. However, the hearing of the whole action could not commence until the pleadings were complete and orders were obtained from Justice Tadgell to produce defences within 14 days. The Council did not deliver its Defence until 21 October. Repeated attempts to have the case listed were then pursued—there were sixteen recorded occasions of communication with the Listing Master's office and various summonses were issued to try and get the case fixed. It was in fact set down before six judges before it finally came on for hearing before Justice O'Bryan! I will not dwell upon the various procedures by which Blake & Riggall sought to get the matter down for the 'earliest possible date'. They are set out in detail in a schedule prepared by Simon Molesworth which I have called the 'Thirty-eight Steps', but the space prevents its reproduction here.

It has been alleged that the residents' advisers did not take adequate steps to get the matter heard.[22] A careful examination of the efforts made indicates that in fact the opposite was the case—the residents and their advisers at all times proceeded with the utmost vigour. Neil Brown has confirmed that Molesworth made every possible effort and adds that he personally took the matter up because of the extensive delays. He even endeavoured to see the Chief Justice, Sir John Young, but he was on leave although Brown did outline the problems to Young's Associate who placed the matter before Sir John on his return. The message came back that, 'there was nothing that he could do'. Brown says that he then pursued it with the Listing Master and in frustration, finally referred the matter to Mr Justice Ormiston who was then chairman of the Bar committee examining the very problem of Supreme Court delays. It was referred on the basis that if they were looking for a good example of unreasonable and continuing delay, then this was it. Looking back on the saga, Brown commented, 'we did everything we could to get the matter on'.[23] Inevitably, delays meant briefing and de-briefing witnesses and a succession of seven barristers. The costs mounted steadily.

The writ was issued on 30 July 1982 and the hearing did not commence until 3 November 1983—a period of 15 months. If the Council had indicated at the outset that there was no possibility of settling the matter, the residents may well have abandoned the case altogether. But Councillors who could see the injustice of the case encouraged the residents to keep the litigation afoot with a view to achieving a negotiated settlement.

In December 1982, the Cain Government removed the Commissioners and restored a democratically elected Melbourne City Council. The residents breathed a sigh of relief believing that at last reason would prevail and the matter would be settled. The Council established a Fitzgibbon Street Committee chaired by Councillor Gordon Moffatt and thereafter Councillor Tom Lynch and it took several positive steps. The residents were invited to address the committee and they argued that inevitably the permit would be held invalid and that consequently it was desirable to settle the matter quickly.

Considerable negotiations did take place, and at one stage the residents were closeted for ten hours at the Blake & Riggall offices while the barristers negotiated, relaying messages back to them to ascertain what might be acceptable. The Council offered the residents 50 per cent of their costs and the Wades $120,000, conditionally upon demolition of the first floor extension. The Wades, in considering this, enquired whether the residents would consent to dropping their opposition to the plans for the front. They replied that they were not even in a position to consent, since in that action there were over forty other objectors, such as the National Trust and the Council, who were also opposed to the Wades. After lengthy delays, Wade declined the settlement which the residents and the Council had agreed upon. That was the end of realistic negotiations. Almost immediately thereafter, the Council realised that its liability was covered by its insurers, Lloyds of London. It therefore invoked the insuress to indemnify it—but not without some soul searching.

Indemnification meant that all responsibility for the matter went out of the Council's hands. It could no longer negotiate or meaningfully discuss the matter. Councillors were advised by Garth Buckner, QC, who now represented the insurers *and* the Council, that any comments they made concerning the case could result in the insurer disclaiming liability. This in turn could mean that any such Councillor might be deemed to have acted negligently and could therefore be sued. The vote to entrust the matter to the insurers was passed by only one. It was a fatal decision because the insurers were consistently to take a hard line and to show little or no interest in settlement. For Lloyds, concerned with long term structural issues of insurance cover only, the costs of litigation were of little moment. The decision also meant that the dogged Garth Buckner now acted for both parties — the Council and the insurer — although their interests at times were far from identical. This may well have had a significant bearing upon many aspects of the case. Time and again at negotiations it was suggested that certain points be conceded as a compromise but the parties were constantly warned that Lloyds, the masters from afar, would void the policy and escape liability altogether if any concessions were made. From the time Lloyds became involved, effective negotiations were crippled. As the State Ombudsman has observed, there are major difficulties associated with indemnity insurance since the company concerned is generally neither interested in the welfare of ratepayers, the justice of the matter nor indeed anything else other than limiting the extent of claims against it.

It should also be mentioned that some Councillors honestly believed that the residents' case was so strong that they must win, and that accordingly, Lloyds would meet all the costs and overall there would be a happy ending to the case.

So unsatisfactory was the arrangement that, after the Supreme Court hearing before Justice O'Bryan, in an effort to break the deadlock the Council sponsored a visit to London by Bethke, Murray, and Councillors Peter Black and Tom Lynch. The trip unfortunately was not successful and Lloyds proved resolute and uncompromising.

While the residents agonised throughout this period the Wades were also busy. Following, their success at the injunction and revocation hearings, they submitted a modified rear plan deleting the sun-deck, which was approved in September 1982. However, in the same month, the Council refused the applications for the front façade and brick fence. In October, the Wades joined Norman Day as a third party seeking indemnity from him (for any losses they might potentially suffer). The Wades also appealed to the Planning Appeals Board against the Council's determination to refuse the permits for the front façade and fence. In October the residents issued a summons and obtained an order for a 'speedy trial'.

In November 1982, Wade was prosecuted at the Melbourne Magistrates Court for carrying out the works at the front without a planning permit. The charge was found proven and the defendant placed on a six-month good behaviour bond and ordered to pay costs of $418.40. In May 1983, the Wades delivered to the Council notice claiming indemnity and in July, Wade was again prosecuted in the same court, this time in connection with the rear trellis fence and again for not having a permit. The charges were again found proven and the defendant placed on a good behaviour bond.

Footnotes

1 Judgement of Justice O'Bryan (Supreme Court of Victoria), *P. Thorne (and Others) v. D. and R. Wade, Councillors and Citizens of the City of Melbourne*, p. 40a.

2 *Ibid*, p. 29a.

3 Letter from Mr Bethke to the Ombudsman, 4 August 1982.

4 Letter from Ian Murray to the Ombudsman, 15 October 1982.

5 Miss Chisholm's second affidavit, p. 3.

6 Resolution of the Council, 28 July 1982.

7 One barrister for the residents said that even if it had been possible to get before Justice Gobbo prior to the foundations being dug, his response would have been the same—i.e. let them build, it is at their risk and the residents are not affected thereby.

8 Simon Molesworth, 'Extract from notes taken at the time of His Honour Mr Justice Gobbo delivering judgement at 2.15 p.m. on Tuesday, 3rd August 1982'.

9 Sid Forsey, 'Transcription of Notes Made at Injunction Attempt before Justice Gobbo'.

10 *Ibid*.

11 *Ibid*.

12 Molesworth, *op. cit.*

13 The *Herald*, 3 August 1982.

14 Molesworth, *op. cit.*

15 Forsey, *op. cit.*

[16] Molesworth, *op. cit.*

[17] Transcript of the hearing of the Supreme Court before Justice O'Bryan, p. 1687.

[18] I have based my description on the following sources: Sid Forsey, 'Transcription of Notes Made at Injunction Attempt before Justice Gobbo' (in many ways the most detailed and accurate record); Simon Molesworth (solicitor for some of the residents), 'Extract from notes taken at the time of His Honour Mr Justice Gobbo delivering judgement at 2.15 p.m. on Tuesday, 3rd August 1982'; 'Note for File', by the author (for the National Trust), 3 August 1982; Loretta Forsey, 'Diary' (lost for over two years but fortuitously discovered by her during my research); the *Sun*, 4 August 1982; the *Age*, 4 August 1982; the *Herald*, 3 August 1982. My research also involved interviews with various other people including barristers and the solicitor acting at that stage for Dr Barbara Falk.

[19] The *Age*, 4 August 1982.

[20] Transcript, *Hearing by Melbourne City Council Commissioners*, 12 August 1982. It should be noted that this was only obtained from the Commissioners following extensive legal pressure over many months.

[21] *Ibid*.

[22] CHERNOV WADES IN, *Victorian Bar News*, Melbourne, Winter, 1985.

[23] From an interview with the author, 23 September 1985.

4
The Supreme Court

Essentially, the issues are legal and must be resolved without regard to social, political or personal considerations.

Justice O'Bryan[1]

If our banner is the Rule of Law, then we cannot be content with a legal system which prides itself on fair substantive laws, but laws which are not, in reality, available for enforcement by the ordinary citizen . . . Lawyers are blamed for the increased likelihood of proceedings in the courts, divorced from the substantial merits of the case.

Justice Kirby[2]

At long last, on 2 November 1983, the dispute concerning the rear extensions finally came on for trial before Justice O'Bryan. The plaintiff residents consisted of the Thornes, the Browns, the Forseys, Dr Falk, Mr Notini and the estate of Miss Chisholm. The defendants were the Wades and the Lord Mayor, Councillors and Citizens of the City of Melbourne. The barristers appearing for the residents were Neil Brown, QC, with Greg Garde; for the Council, Garth Buckner, QC, and Chris Canavan; and for the Wades, Tom Neesham, QC. The case ran for a total of 26 days (24 hearing days straight, one for the costs hearing and one for the judgement).

Neil Brown was the sixth barrister to become involved for the residents. He accepted the brief rather late in the saga because he felt the issues warranted his involvement although his normal field is industrial law — frequently appearing before the Arbitration Commission. He is very much the rounded man with interests in the arts and environment. He is a consummate politician. During the Fraser years he held several portfolios and with the Liberal leadership spill in September 1985, nearly two years after the hearing, Brown suddenly shot

Doug and Raelene Wade during court proceedings. Courtesy the *Age*.

into prominence again by appointment to the position of deputy to leader John Howard, who replaced Andrew Peacock.

Justice O'Bryan upheld the residents, primary contention that the permit for the extensions was 'null and void'. However, he declined to provide relief since he did not believe it was:

> ... equitable ... now or in the future ... In my opinion, in the light of the findings I have made, I would never contemplate granting a mandatory injunction against the Wades in relation to the additions and alterations made to the Wade house authorised by permit CM 5032. I am perfectly satisfied that the Wades acted in good faith at all material times and proceeded with the additions and alterations in the reasonable belief that they were legally entitled to do so. The mere fact that the plaintiffs contended otherwise and *issued a writ does not mean that the Wades acted unwisely or took a calculated risk* in refusing to desist from completing the works. The Wades had engaged a reputable, independent contractor in Norman Day, to advise them as to building matters and to apply for all necessary permits. They could not be expected to know that the relevant authority would grant an invalid planning permit. (author's italics)

While the residents had found this a bitter pill to swallow, insult was heaped upon injury when the judge ordered the residents to pay not merely all the Wades' costs, but all their own and half the Council's, despite their success on what the judge described as the 'main issue' and despite the fact that the Council had clearly erred in issuing the invalid permit. The residents had been told of the risks but no one could have contemplated the severity of the result.

In essence the residents' case claimed the permit was invalid. They brought this to the attention of the Council at an early stage when rectification was practicable and an application for a valid permit could have been lodged by the Wades. Such an application, they said, would have enabled any aggrieved resident to object and if necessary, for the matter to be resolved on the town planning merits in the normal manner before the Appeals Board. They claimed that for the Wades to have gone on building in defiance of the litigation could only be seen as an attempt to pre-empt the normal planning processes and that no one should place themselves above the law and advance their position by continuing to build without a valid permit. For their part, the Wades simply ignored the protests so far as they could, went on with their building and claimed that once a permit is issued, the holder is entitled to presume its validity until proved otherwise.

The remedies sought by the residents included a declaration that the permit was null and void, an injunction requiring the defendants to remove and make good the second storey extension or alternatively, damages. The residents chose not to sue the Council for negligence although this may well have succeeded. However, this would only have yielded damages and this was not a priority.

The attack rested upon several grounds. It was first claimed that the Council's Interim Development Order permit was not valid because it had been issued by the Council after it failed to comply with s. 18B of the Planning Act; secondly, a second permit—this time under the Melbourne and Metropolitan Planning Scheme—had not been sought or obtained; and thirdly, that the I.D.O. permit was invalid because it had been obtained by misrepresentation; and fourthly, the I.D.O. permit was incorrectly issued since by law, it should have been issued by the Town Clerk. The principal attack, however, focussed upon s. 18B where, as we have seen, the Council had already received advice from its own independent consultant Lawrie Wilson to the effect that the permit was in breach of the Act and therefore invalid.

Invalidity of the Permit—Lack of Notice

Section 18B(1) of the Act requires that:

> Where the Council is of the opinion that the grant of a permit may cause a *substantial detriment* to any person other than the applicant, [it] . . . shall not determine to grant the permit unless it first does one or other of the following . . . namely, to ensure that appropriate notice is given, to such person(s) in such manner and within such time as the authority specifies . . . [etc.] (author's italics)

Accordingly, the judge said that John Noonan, the Council's Acting Chief Planner, was required to make the critical decision and form an opinion as to whether the proposal, 'may cause a substantial detriment to any person other than

64

the applicant'. This was then, as the judge found, the 'main issue', since if the Council had failed in its statutory duty, then the permit would be invalid and the extensions therefore illegal.

The application had initially lain upon the desk of Lucy Liew in the planning department for some time. At this point, pressure was applied, 'from above', to have the matter expedited although it is difficult to understand what the hurry was, since the Wades did not in fact commence work until some time in April 1982. It was the Wades who initiated the pressure just as they had with the Appeals Board.

Wade contacted the Town Clerk 'to find out why it was taking so long . . . [although the application had only been lodged for] . . . probably over a week or two weeks . . . he said he would follow it up . . . He said he'd passed it over to Mr Williams, I believe, or Mr Noonan . . .'[3] The instruction went out that the matter be dealt with 'A.S.A.P.'. It is understood that there was in fact a card with this instruction placed on the file but it subsequently disappeared. This was not lost upon Justice O'Bryan who commented, 'It was unfortunate that the application was processed so close to Christmas *with considerable pressure imposed upon planning officers* about to take their Christmas leave . . .'[4] (author's italics)

The judge was highly critical of the absence of adequate procedures for Council officers processing applications and took the view that when in doubt as to whether detriment might be caused, the Council should err on the safe side and advertise although this might well be inconvenient as suggested by the Council's witnesses. The judge was extremely critical of the Council's lack of criteria and prescribed minimum information standards:

> . . . I see no reason why a responsible authority should not require, in the case of every proposal, to alter or add to a building above the ground floor level, that an elevation plan must accompany the application. It should not be left to the discretion of the town planner processing the application to seek out information which one might regard as basic and essential to a full and proper appreciation of a proposal.[5]

The application was passed to John Keaney who stated that he undertook a site inspection, although it transpired that he did not actually enter the land. Justice O'Bryan suggested that if he had spoken to Notini or Chisholm,

> At least he might have learned whether they understood the extent of the works at the rear and whether there were other persons owning or occupying the premises who might be caused substantial detriment. None of that was done however.[6]

The judge examined the report of Keaney and highlighted the confusion inherent in the Council's assessment:

> *The work proposed at the rear of the Wade house was of a very substantial nature*, extending across the whole width of the land and involving a two-storey extension to an existing row house. The omission to refer to this aspect of the proposed work is curious and creates a suspicion in my mind, that *Keaney either did not fully appreciate the plan specified a substantial addition at the rear of the house, or he misread the plan* . . . Keaney actually never addressed his mind to the question of whether any person, other than Miss Chisholm or Notini, may be caused a substantial detriment if permits were granted . . . An inference should be drawn that Keaney's report was hastily prepared on the eve of Christmas.[7] (author's italics)

It was clear from the evidence that Keaney had not appreciated the magnitude of the extensions and therefore was not able to assess the impact of its bulk and of overlooking and over-shadowing. His report described the works as to 'substantially renovate' and he explained that, 'The internal workings of the house in my opinion as a planning consideration was not all that relevant'.[8] It may be that this appreciation may have caused the Town Clerk not to refer to extensions at all when he wrote to the Ombudsman describing the proposal on 4 August 1982. The judge concluded that Keaney was in-experienced and was left largely to his own devices.

Keaney completed his report on Christmas Eve and it was then passed to his supervisor Bolger, who apparently failed to consider the issue of substantial detriment further and on the very same day, forwarded it to John Noonan, the Deputy City Planner. The pressure was mounting.

Following extensive cross-examination, the judge was to conclude that Noonan was 'distracted by the consents'[9] (being the signatures of the adjoining neighbours on the plans shown to them by Wade), and that this affected Noonan's earlier

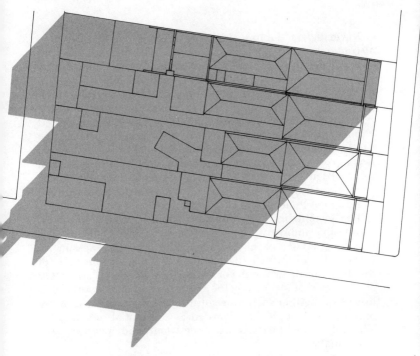

A highlighted shadow diagram illustrating the extent of mid-winter shadow caused by the extensions. From court exhibit by Dr Mark Sholtis, University of Melbourne.

assessment that there would in fact be substantial detriment to neighbours, who accordingly should have been notified under s. 18B. The residents stated at the hearing that Noonan had believed that the works were confined to 'refurbishing of the existing walls inside' and Noonan at least partly confirmed this in his evidence when he referred to his discussion with Loretta Forsey: 'But I remember denying at the time that it was a 25-foot high wall on the south boundary. This is the one thing that sticks in my mind with respect to that conversation'.[10] Loretta Forsey also recalls Noonan not being able to 'understand why this figure of 25 feet was being bandied around. He just couldn't understand where that came from. A twenty-five-foot wall being put up'.[11]

Nevertheless, the judge managed to conclude that 'Noonan also understood the proposals for the rear of the house and was not deceived or misled'.[12] Noonan had concluded that since Notini and Chisholm had signed the plans, it could therefore be assumed that no one would suffer substantial detriment. An unfortunate leap in logic. The judge held that it was this mistaken emphasis upon the consents which caused Noonan to wrongly believe that no substantial detriment would be caused. Having reached this conclusion, he decided (wrongly) that he would not need to advertise the application in accordance with s. 18B — this was a fatal error and so the permit was null and void. The residents had succeeded on the first limb of their attack.

The second limb was also won when it was held that no responsible authority (Council) could have formed the opinion that the grant of a permit may not cause substantial detriment. It was held, following expert evidence, that at various times of the year the Brown and Forsey gardens would be adversely affected by shadows cast by the extension and that, 'appreciable loss of sunlight at such times of the year is significant, in my opinion, and might be regarded as substantial detriment'.[13] The judge concluded his searching twenty-four-page analysis of the matter:

> In my opinion it is almost beyond argument that the bulk appearance of the high wall on the southern boundary of the Wade house, is a matter of substantial detriment to the owners of both the Brown and Forsey homes. This must have been obvious and foreseeable to any competent town planner in December 1981.
>
> In my opinion, *the bulk appearance of the extension and the loss of privacy caused by overlooking, are matters which seriously impair Notini's enjoyment of his small garden area.* I consider therefore, no reasonable [Council] could in the circumstances, have formed the opinion in December 1981, that no substantial detriment might be caused by the proposals . . . It follows that the Council was in breach of its obligations under s. 18B and the permit granted by Noonan is null and void.[14] (author's italics)

The residents had convincingly succeeded in proving that the permit was invalid and that they had suffered substantial detriment under s. 18B. This was unprecedented and no mean feat.

The Melbourne and Metropolitan Planning Scheme

> The different results also tend to show the absurdity of the whole exercise in terms of whether or not a permit was required.
> *Justice O'Bryan*[15]

The application for a permit was not processed under the Planning Scheme, possibly because the Council officers believed one was not required. Clause 7(1)(d)(iii) of the Scheme provided that,

> where land is used other than for a detached house or any of the purposes specified in sub-paragraph (ii) hereof the floor area of any building existing on the land at such date *shall not be increased* and no *new building shall be constructed* without the permission of the responsible authority . . . (author's italics)

The residents claimed that an additional permit was required under the Planning Scheme because the floor area was to be increased and because a new building was to be constructed. The judge observed of the Planning Scheme, that it was 'confusing, contradictory, full of ambiguities and inconsistencies. It must be a nightmare to administer and a paradise for lawyers'.

The court met with acute problems of interpretation, the subclause being 'unhappily drafted and ambiguous'. One might have supposed, as their consultant Wilson had suggested, that where there was doubt, the Council should properly err on the safe side, and require that a permit be applied for. However, the judge took a contrary view and held that where there was, 'ambiguity or doubt created by the definition of "floor area", [it] should be resolved in favour of the persons alleged guilty of wrongdoing, in accordance with the ordinary principles of construction of a penal provision; in this case in favour of Mr and Mrs Wade'.[16]

The issue boiled down to whether or not there had been an increase of floor area and also a dispute of semantics as to whether there was a 'new building'. The evidence was highly conflicting, there being a variety of plans and of experts who undertook measurements. There was also the vexed question of whether the Wades could take advantage of including the shanty illegal buildings when calculating the existing floor space. The residents said that the Wades should not benefit from inclusion of the illegal works erected by the previous owner, but the judge held that the Wades were not to know they were illegal. The structures included a garage, three bird cages and an open-sided bar entertainment area. The judge held that the garage should be excluded from the existing 'floor area' while the rest could be included.

Examination of the various calculations proved immensely complex and time consuming and the judge commented that, 'The different results tend to show the absurdity of the whole exercise in terms of whether or not a permit was required'.[17] No less than eight experts gave evidence, of which five were taken seriously.

The judge considered evidence from one of the Council's experts — Kamenev — as the most accurate and on this basis held that the application did not require a permit. He omitted to deal with the second issue of whether the work constituted 'new building', despite lengthy argument by respective counsel. The conclusion, adverse to the residents, has surprised observers since it is now not clear what meaning, if any, is added by the words, 'new building'. An amendment has been proposed to rectify the effect of the judgement.

It might be argued that the finding was of little consequence, since in the first place the residents had proved that the only permit held was invalid, and further, even if they had succeeded on the Planning Scheme issue, the judge would still have the power to ignore the requirement in exercising his discretion in relation to remedies. However, the winning and losing of such issues was to become important in relation to the question of costs.

Authorisation to Issue the Permit

The actual permit was signed by D. A. Goodwin, the Deputy City Planner (statutory) who had been delegated authority to issue such permits by the Council in April 1981. However, the residents were able to establish that the Council had exceeded its powers and that legally, permits must be signed by the Municipal Clerk or secretary. It had taken months for the Council to disclose the instrument of delegation authorising

Goodwin. How can it be justifiable to shroud such a document in secrecy? Neil Brown, counsel for the residents, had argued that this was a substantial, not merely technical matter, but the judge held that the 'departure from the prescribed form is a mere insubstantial, procedural, irregularity which does not vitiate the permit'.[18]

Participation in Planning ('Standing' or *locus standi*)

> Of course your Honour, this case is not concerned with natural justice.
>
> *Garth Buckner, QC*

> On the contrary Mr Buckner, it is, these people have sought to be heard and they have never been heard.
>
> *Justice O'Bryan*

It was critical to resolve who had legal standing (that is, the right to come to court as a party and seek its assistance). This right also derives from s. 18B(1) of the Act. Justice O'Bryan held that to have standing, one must be able to prove a 'special interest' that went beyond matters of 'mere intellectual or emotional concern'. He said that while it was not necessary to prove 'actual monetary loss', the individual must prove a 'significant loss of amenity within his land'.

Dr Falk, who lives immediately to the rear of the Wade house across a narrow right of way, was held to lack the requisite 'special interest' because, 'Whilst it is true that the Falk house is more prone to be overlooked from the second storey rear windows of the Wade house since the sunroom was built, the effect of overlooking does not, in my opinion, constitute serious diminution in the amenity enjoyed by Doctor Falk within her property'. This finding was made despite the assessments of diminution of property value of approximately $7500 provided by a firm of sworn valuers. The Thornes at number 11 were also denied standing on the basis that they would not suffer a serious loss of amenity.

The three surrounding properties, owned by the Notinis, the Browns and the Forseys, suffered sufficient detriment (overshadowing, bulk appearance, loss of privacy, etc.) to demonstrate a 'special interest . . . [and have] suffered damage by reason of the grant of the permit'. These residents were accordingly held to have standing before the court.

Justice O'Bryan found that they had standing due to their loss of amenity although he was reluctant to concede diminution in money value which was difficult to assess, 'in the absence of sales experience'. Of course, it need hardly be pointed out that there have been few examples similar to the Wades which might provide an historical trend. Nevertheless, the loss of amenity was substantial and Justice O'Bryan found:

> I believe that Dr and Mrs Brown's aspirations for the future use and enjoyment of their home have been dealt a severe blow by the additions at the rear of the Wade house. *It is really a disaster for them*, in that a considerable portion of the view enjoyed to the north both from the garden and from the second storey window at the rear of their home has now been lost. Considerable overshadowing in the garden has occurred and the bulk appearance of the southern wall is unsightly.[19] (author's italics)

The decision represented another important win against the Wades since Neesham, with some support from Buckner, had claimed that none of the residents had proved the 'necessary damage peculiar to his or her situation'.[20]

The implications of the decision are very significant, however, and will result in radical changes concerning rights of appearance before the Board. It means that certainly in relation to run of the mill developments within residential areas, very few people will now be capable of demonstrating the requisite 'special interest'. Already, I am told, the Council has in some cases decided not to inform residents of housing alterations/additions, should they be separated from the subject land by a mere right of way—as was Dr Falk.

The legal position has now been clearly stated. Environmental lawyers believe that originally the Act was deliberately cast so that it could be interpreted widely in the light of changing conditions and social expectations. The decision, it is argued, abandons the broad discretionary practices of the past in favour of a more rigid common law test, which provides greater clarity but at the cost of flexibility. Past practices requiring regular advertising, notification, etc., may increasingly be dropped save in the more obvious cases. Until

Doug Wade talking to reporters. The residents were not the only ones to use the media to explain their position. Courtesy the *Age*.

Evan Walker, Minister for Planning and the Environment.

'I believe that Dr and Mrs Brown's aspirations for the future use and enjoyment of their home have been dealt a severe blow by the additions at the rear of the Wade house. It really is a disaster for them' (Justice O'Bryan). Here Ken Brown expresses impotent rage. Courtesy *News Limited*.

now, it has generally been assumed (certainly by the Appeals Board and Councils throughout Victoria), that groups and residents who 'lived near by', should be allowed to participate in the planning processes in the wider community interest, both in terms of town planning considerations and accountability.

In passing, it may be fair to observe that the decision appears to coincide with recent trends in government, legal and political circles—to limit opportunities for ordinary people to participate in the planning processes. Accordingly, where a Council decides not to notify individuals or the public at large of a development and issues a permit as in the Wade Case, it will be a bold resident indeed who seeks redress before the courts since the onus will rest squarely upon him to prove that the Council erred and that he should have been notified. Councils now know that in the majority of cases, no residents would be foolish or wealthy enough to challenge their action.

In a recent decision at Lorne, local residents were deprived of an opportunity to object to the Cumberland Development when the Winchelsea Shire issued a permit without notifying anyone. The development includes 16 shops, 100 residential units, recreational facilities, a theatre and 170 car spaces!

The Fait Accompli

Any step the [Wades] take from this point on they take at their peril.

Justice Gobbo

The mere fact that the residents . . . issued a writ does not mean that the Wades acted unwisely or took a calculated risk in refusing to desist.

Justice O'Bryan[21]

At various times during this case, I have been suddenly struck by *Alice in Wonderland* notions of unreality linked on occasions with certain sinister overtones which Carrick Chambers adverted to at an early stage. The law concludes that should you have an invalid permit, then build as fast as you can, since the more you do before the law catches up, then the easier it will be to demonstrate the detriment you must suffer should anyone protest that the public law should be observed. The law positively encourages illegality!

Extraordinary though it may seem, Justice O'Bryan clearly was not informed in any detail of the warnings and assurances given by Justice Gobbo. Certainly he never fully appreciated the effect of them. Indeed, it is said that when the matter was subsequently raised with Justice Gobbo himself, the latter was unable to recall the issue in detail. Obviously, something needs to be done about the inadequate recording services in the Practice Court. While full recording services are expensive, simple cassette recordings should suffice to enable a transcript to be made at a later date should this ever be required. (Senior counsel have agreed with me that this would be a most useful reform.) As explained in chapter 3, there was no court transcript but there was certainly abundant evidence of the proceedings. Unfortunately for the residents, their key barristers had not been privy to Justice Gobbo's warnings. Neil Brown did seek to raise the matter in a roundabout way with Justice O'Bryan at the outset of the case, but the thrust of the warning, that it was the Wades, who 'proceeded at their own risk' (on one occasion he used the word 'peril'), and that the residents would not be disadvantaged by the non-issue of the injunction, simply did not come across. Brown raised it with the judge in this way:

MR BROWN: No injunction was granted, no, and that is apparent from the order. But what is significant Your Honour and I will at some stage draw it to your Honour's attention in some detail. It is a fairly significant matter. There may be a dispute about it and I have not drawn it to the attention of my learned friends, but Justice Gobbo made remarks on that occasion, Your Honour.

HIS HONOUR: His remarks will not be in any way subject of a decision which binds me.

MR BROWN: Well Your Honour, with respect, we would argue that they would, because they constitute in effect, a warning from the court, that there are remedies available to plaintiffs to pursue their remedies in this case, if these works proceeded with and if they reach a conclusion. In other words, we say that it is one, although not of course the only factor which should be taken into account in considering Your Honour's discretionary powers to grant an injunction. We say, of course, the ... defendants ... were warned by the correspondence.

HIS HONOUR: Surely the writ itself is the caveat?

MR BROWN: And the writ is the warning, Your Honour, with respect. I agree with that. But we say that the warnings we gave by the letters, the warnings we gave by the proceedings ...

HIS HONOUR: What, was it made apparent publicly? I mean in the Court. Why the interlocutory injunction did not proceed? ... I do not follow what His Honour said on that occasion in any way binds me in this proceeding.

MR BROWN: It does not bind you, Your Honour, I am not putting that it binds you ... the injunction ... is one of the factors that Your Honour should have regard to, is the degree and nature of the composite warnings which were given to the defendants ... Gobbo J giving in effect, a warning that if the works went on, if they were completed, ... no one should assume that simply because the works were completed, that the building was up, that it was going to stay up forever, because there were remedies which were open to the plaintiff ...

HIS HONOUR: If I may say so, I would have thought that was obvious enough, Mr Brown.

MR BROWN: ... But it is one factor, Your Honour. It was, in fact, a factor mentioned in *Day v. Pinglen*, the case which I mentioned ...

HIS HONOUR: I follow what you say.

MR BROWN: ... that decision ... we would say is some authority for the proposition that a Court in the situation in which Your Honour now is can have regard to that part of the history. But that is the way it is put, Your Honour, simply as some of the factors which Your Honour would be entitled to take into account in considering the exercise of discretion.

I have quoted in some detail from the transcript because the passage neatly illustrates the unsatisfactory manner in which the submission proceeded. It is fair to say, with the benefit of hindsight, that the argument was loosely advanced—first, it binds His Honour, then it doesn't—and ultimately it was merely put as one which the judge is 'entitled to take into account in considering the exercise of discretion'.

The principles set out by the High Court case of *Day v. Pinglen* are barely advanced, where a, 'decision [was made] to proceed to completion of the said building, and . . . to have it completed by the time the appeal had been disposed of . . .'[22] These could almost have been Justice Gobbo's words! There was then, no real elaboration of the principle, namely that an individual may not advance his position by deliberately continuing to build in the face of a challenge to the validity of the permit nor any explanation of Justice Gobbo's view that there was no need to act to avoid the residents' position being eroded.

Unfortunately, the history of Justice Gobbo's warnings, and the significance of the many other warnings was not developed adequately and His Honour seemed quite comfortable with the view that the Wades had *not* taken a 'calculated risk'.

In responding to Brown the judge says that, 'the writ itself is the caveat' (that is, warning, admonition, caution—O.E.D.), but in his judgement he concludes that the mere issue of 'a writ does not mean that the Wades acted unwisely or took a calculated risk'. The propositions are in conflict and it is a conflict which is never satisfactorily resolved and which only serves to create confusion, particularly before the Full Court.

The critical issue before the court which was not analysed concerned the state of mind of the Wades. Did they in fact take a risk in proceeding? Justice O'Bryan does not begin to get to grips with the question. Can it seriously be put that just because the Wades *may* have believed they had a valid permit, that therefore they were not taking a risk in proceeding? Surely, even if they did believe they had a valid permit, their professional advisers would have warned them in their discussions of the risks, bearing in mind also, the conclusion of His Honour, that '*no reasonable responsible authority could in the circumstances, have formed the opinion in December 1981, that no substantial detriment might be caused.* It follows that the Council was in breach of its obligations under s. 18B and the permit granted by Noonan was null and void'. (author's italics)

A more searching analysis would have been appropriate although the warnings by Justice Gobbo alone could well have been sufficient to attract the rule in *Day v. Pinglen*. Remember, too, the first warnings came prior to commencement of the rear construction. The residents, on learning of the grant of the permit, immediately took the matter up with the Wades, the Commissioners and the relevant Ministers. The Wades were promptly warned in writing by three firms of solicitors acting for the various residents, that the matter would be pursued at law if necessary.

The writ then, may indeed have been the 'caveat' as the judge said, but the Wades had already been well and truly warned — the seeking of an injunction was further evidence of the residents' determination to have the matter tested and the revocation proceedings raised the gravest doubts concerning the validity of the permit. Council staff had recommended that it be revoked, the Commissioners announced their intention to revoke and Wilson, the Council's independent consultant, had also confirmed that in his view the permit was invalid. There was, in short, tremendous uncertainty and opposition at many levels. How could it possibly be argued that the Wades did not take a 'risk', in the sense put to them by Justice Gobbo? It seems beyond argument that the Wades would have conferred with their advisers at various stages and doubtless, as on other occasions, they resolved to take their chances, on the assumption that 'activity is nine-tenths of the law'.

If necessary, the analysis could have gone further and considered the history of Wade's actions immediately prior to the disputed works. Could it be said that he was the kind of man who would proceed in the face of 'risks'? Consider the following facts, which are not in dispute:

1. The work to the front brick fence proceeded at an extra-ordinarily rapid pace involving seven bricklayers. Why? Is it not relevant that Wade did *not* have a permit, and that perhaps he figured the work might be allowed to stay, if only he could get it up quickly enough?

Wade admitted in evidence that Bethke had told him there was a problem with the permit and a meeting was convened at the Town Hall on Saturday 5 June 1982 at which Bethke confirmed Wade did not have a valid permit. For Wade it had been a race against the clock which he had won, in the sense that the fence was furiously completed the day before. On the other hand, his attempt to pre-empt the planning process failed to the extent that he was successfully prosecuted by the Council.

77

2. It could be argued that the Wades adopted a similar attitude concerning the demolition of the wing walls and verandah.

3. Norman Day gave about twenty people, in my presence, an assurance that work to the front would cease pending clarification of whether a valid permit existed. No such permit existed, as we have seen, but the work proceeded nevertheless. By this time, of course, the Council had been alerted and on 22 October 1982, the Town Clerk wrote to the Wades telling them that the work was in breach of the Act and that 'until approval is given, development of the façade must not be commenced [and] . . . You are hereby advised that unless such development ceases forthwith, legal proceedings will be instituted'. Was Day or Wade responsible for these continued illegal works? Day wrote to Wade's solicitor Bill Carroll making his position clear on the very same day:

> The Wades plan to have the builder install their façade windows from inside the house tomorrow and I assume from what they tell me that you have given them advice that they may do so. My advice to them is that the matter is a legal one and one I am not qualified to make.
>
> From what I have seen to date I cannot predict the reaction of the Council nor the local groups and I have told Raeline [*sic*] that is my opinion, today.

Despite these warnings, Wade did proceed with further works in response to which he was twice successfully prosecuted by the Council. To be fair to the Wades, they continued work to the windows, they said, to make the building waterproof. But why not negotiate a proposal instead of charging ahead only to be prosecuted?

4. The fact that the Wades should persist with Day's plans for the façade and front fence in the light of the long history of the area as a conservation precinct, the new planning controls, the refusal by the Council to issue a permit, and the opposition of the neighbours, Parkville Association, the National Trust, independent Council consultants, etc., surely says something about their preparedness to risk litigation?

5. The Wades declined to accept negotiated settlements, three of which had been agreed to by the other parties after extensive discussions. It was Wade who ultimately walked away from the conference table after the other parties reached agreement.

6. The Wades also chanced their arm by initiating proceedings in the Supreme Court against the Council in an unsuccessful endeavour to have the revocation proceedings stopped.

Finally, it was ironical that virtually the same issue arose again at the Appeals Board, as we have seen. It reached a contrary conclusion, namely that a person's position could *not* be advanced by continued construction without a valid permit. In that instance, the Board was primarily concerned to consider the appropriateness of the Day/Wade proposal in the town planning context. It should be noted that the detriment sustained by the Wades in proceeding was quite substantial. They had sunk an estimated $8000 on the illegal building works and an estimated $27,000 in legal and advisers' fees in connection with the hearing, but the Board did *not* permit such matters to be advanced in the Wades' favour. To be fair, the two cases are not precisely identical since in one case no permit existed, while in the other, one did exist but was invalid. Nevertheless, the analogy is accurate to the extent that the Wades were aware in both cases, given a reasonable consideration of the matter, that the legality of the work being undertaken was very seriously in issue and under legal challenge.

If one accepts, as some observers have, that Justice O'Bryan had decided that the best way of resolving the dilemma (of who should suffer where both sides were innocent) was to leave the building there and to halt further litigation; then we can better comprehend the way in which he reached his conclusions. Neil Brown had already put the High Court case of *Day v. Pinglen* to the judge and he rejected the suggestion that the Wades had deliberately advanced their position by taking a calculated risk. Because of that finding he was not bound by the principles enunciated in *Day v. Pinglen*.

Accordingly, he found that the Wades had proceeded in ignorance of any risk. With hindsight we can now see how the thrust of the arguments was not really addressed by the court. Brown had said to the judge that it was a matter to which he would return 'in some detail'. But he did not since he was disheartened by his reception. The submission was not strongly mounted, no evidence was led concerning Justice Gobbo's warnings and the judge's response was such that Brown resolved not to come back for more.

Given that Justice Gobbo was not disposed to proceed with the injunction hearing, I cannot cavil with his enunciation of the legal position although it should have been recorded in some fashion. In those circumstances, I can agree with Justice Gobbo when he warned the Wades that to continue building would be 'at their own peril'. It was at their own peril; it was a long high kick for goal, and this time it paid off.

If the Wade house case proves nothing else, it proves that to become involved in the courts is to 'proceed at your own peril'.

Misrepresentation

It is at this point that Day takes off on to a plane of . . . unreality . . .

Miles Lewis[23]

No elevation plans were prepared at the outset . . . The full extent of the structure might not be appreciated by anyone other than an architect.

Justice O'Bryan[24]

The thrust of the residents' case as set out in their statement of claim was that the grant of permit CM 5032 for the rear extensions was in breach of s. 18B and that they should, therefore, have been given an opportunity to object. As indicated, they were unclear as to the decision making processes by which Council had issued the permit and accordingly made alternative claims. They said that if the Council had formed the opinion that no substantial detriment would result, then that opinion was due to the misleading and inaccurate plans which failed to adequately indicate what was proposed.

The residents alleged that the Council could have formed its opinion due to the misrepresentations made by Wade which induced Notini and Chisholm to sign their consents to the plans. They alleged that Wade had said that he would 'restore the house to its original condition' and that at no stage did he disclose that it was proposed to construct a substantial rear two-storey extension with sun-deck which would reach across to the side boundaries.

However, the judge totally rejected the allegations of mis-representation although he accepted that the plans were clearly inadequate. The plans lodged at the Council by Day did not include elevations although the extensions were partly coloured to show additions. Even so, the judge found that, 'The full extent of the structure proposed at the rear might not be appreciated by anyone other than an architect'. The duplicate plans, such as those presented to Notini, Miss Chisholm and others like Trevor Huggard, were not coloured to indicate the extensions. Even John Noonan, the Acting City Planner, initially told the residents that the works to the rear were confined to within the existing single storey walls.[25]

The plans provided no information concerning the height or relationship of the extensions with neighbouring properties. The plans were inconsistent regarding the rear wall, the area near the southern wall was shown as single storey and had not been coloured as new works, and a skylight shown at ground floor level appeared to indicate that only one storey was proposed. This latter inference was confirmed, at least in the view of the Council's consultant Wilson, by the 'site plan where an apparent parapet wall is indicated extending beyond the existing upper level roof structure on to the proposed sunroom'.

The residents maintained that the plans failed to indicate adequately that a substantial two-storey extension was proposed measuring some 10.5 metres in height and being a third the length of the existing building. (I believe that the figure of 10.5 metres may be an over-estimate. It is, however, the height adopted by the judge and I have used it for the purpose of exposition. These are the inevitable problems which result from inadequate plans.) The relative scale of the structure may be gauged by reflecting upon the fact that it ran from boundary to boundary right across the rear of the property and was significantly higher than the width (6 metres) of the respective properties. Imagine, in relative terms, a standard suburban block with an 18-metre frontage. Behind the house, locate a brick extension running across the rear from boundary to boundary standing 31.5 metres high! Would the neighbours scream? Clearly, Day had a duty to identify the new work and its potential impact to the Council and to anyone likely to be affected. What better way than to disclose the elevations and the three-dimensional model?

At the hearing, Day conceded errors in the drawings but claimed that it was normal for him to proffer a minimum of information: 'You're testing the water with as little document- ation as will be required for the particular case', said Day. The judge noted the 'paucity and inaccuracy of the information supplied', commenting, 'Some of the fault must attach to the [Council]'. He went on to stress that Council officers should have written guidelines indicating the type of information, including elevations, which should be required of applicants.

No one could argue with the judge's findings concerning the need for the Council to tighten up its procedures. What is surprising, however, is that he makes no real criticism of Day as the Wades' architect. The residents had carefully considered citing Day as a defendant, but decided against it because the remedy sought was primarily against the Wades, for an injunction to make good the rear. The residents also believed that the Wades would be responsible for Day's actions as their agent. The Wades had joined Day as a co-defendant (third party) but just prior to the hearing, after discussion between Wade and Day's lawyers, the third party proceedings were dropped. We will never know the reason. This was a clever tactic but unfortunate from the residents' viewpoint since the judge treated Day as an independent contractor, not as Wade's agent, and accordingly, since Day was no longer a party, the residents were required to focus upon Wade and the Council.

Day's professional responsibilities were very real. He knew that his plans must satisfy several purposes. They must meet the Council's planning criteria which include consideration of whether the building will overlook, overshadow, etc., but they must also be adequate to enable the Council to assess whether the development may cause substantial detriment to neighbours, in which case, it *must* notify neighbours under the Act. The inadequacy of the plans to reveal what was proposed in terms of volume, height, proximity, etc., prevented an adequate assessment being made. I believe Day had a moral and professional duty both to his clients and to his profession to clearly reveal what was proposed, to enable the Council to make its assessment in accordance with its statutory responsibilities.

Was Day merely, 'testing the water'? His strategy was simple. He had a client in a hurry who wanted approval for a building and Day anticipated from the beginning there could be trouble. Day submitted as little information as possible hoping it would slip through the planning process while Wade undertook to get the neighbours' consent. Day then took out a form of insurance by approaching Trevor Huggard to act as engineering consultant, because of Huggard's known sensitivity to conservation issues which meant, he assumed, that if there were problems, Huggard would be well placed to deal with them.

Huggard was no fool and initially refused to be involved with Day, but finally agreed under pressure from Wade. Huggard eventually withdrew his services through dissatisfaction with Day. Subsequently, when Day sought to defend his position in the *Age* he quoted Huggard's involvement in an attempt to buttress his own position. Huggard was furious and wrote a disclaimer to the *Age* and instructed his solicitor to write to Day telling him that if he failed to desist from implicating him, he would be sued for defamation. Day desisted.

Day also sought to implicate conservation architect Nigel Lewis on his behalf and on 9 June 1982 went to Lewis' office to discuss the front of the Wade house. At that meeting, Day tabled yet another plan showing a 'façade design with an iron picket fence rather than a brick fence and with a façade that did not feature the cement floral garlands . . .'[27] Day's design criteria subsequently referred to the meeting and Lewis felt that Day was seeking to create the impression that he (Day) 'is either following my advice or that I concur with his approach'.[28] Lewis stated that in fact he regarded the proposal as, 'one of the most threatening precedents to the conservation of this important area . . .'[29] The surfacing of varying plans therefore created considerable confusion throughout the case and the reader will recall the very first meeting between Day and the residents which we touched upon in chapter two.

Although Justice O'Bryan found the plans inadequate to describe the proposal, he declined to hold that Day deliberately sought to deceive. Day's methods confused everyone. Once he obtained a permit for a plan, he added and subtracted sections and then took further copies. In this way, he produced a variety of plans, some displaying Council permit stamps and some without. It is not alleged here that Day produced these collages deliberately to deceive but it certainly caused confusion. The court heard evidence that on various occasions, Day presented plans which he said were approved, when in fact they were not.

Nor is it being alleged here that the building as constructed is seriously at variance from the endorsed plan at the Town Hall. But the plan that Day had approved by the Council did not indicate works to the façade or to the front fence, nor did the plan shown to Mr Notini and Miss Chisholm reproduced on page 44 which bears her signature of consent. But the plans shown to the residents at the initial meeting at the Thornes did show works to the façade and fence and so did the ones shown to Nigel Lewis and to me.

When I interviewed Day at his office on 16 September 1985, he said emphatically that he *still* believed he had a valid permit for the façade and front fence! I said that I could not see how this could possibly be correct since Doug Wade was successfully prosecuted for not having a permit and further-more, Neesham in the Supreme Court conceded that the Wades did not have a permit. To my amazement, Day then produced a plan in support of his contention, clearly stamped with the Council's permit CM 5032 and indicating a proposed curved indented brick fence and for work to be done to the façade. How, I wondered, could Day possess plans, bearing the official permit stamp, which varied from those plans at the Town Hall? The conundrum is explained only by appreciating that the plans are a collage achieved by taping a new front section on to the left hand side and a new 'site plan' to the bottom. The plan reproduced on page 44 is a collage of three plans; the additions can be clearly identified since lines remain where additional sections have been taped over the copy of the original endorsed plan prior to copying.

One conclusion we could draw is that for much of the time, Day simply confused himself. There were too many plans and he was too clever by half. It is the only conclusion which can explain why Day would show me the collage claiming it to be the endorsed plan. I put this question to Dr Lewis who commented that it is impossible to tell, since 'it is at this point that Day takes off on to a plane of unreality . . .'

Such an explanation also provides the key to Doug Wade's

reaction when I accused him of building illegally—which caused him to instruct Buckner to sue me for libel. He doubtless accepted Day's claim to possession of a valid permit for the front and may have been shown the plan which Day showed to the residents and to me. How Wade would have received Day's explanation subsequently, when he was prosecuted for building without a permit, remains a tantalising question. Perhaps it was at this point that Day was joined as a third party defendant by the Wades?

In the result, the judge grew impatient with the varying plans and Day was exonerated with the comment that even if Day were guilty of false representations, 'there is not a tittle of evidence which implicates either Mr or Mrs Wade in such wrongdoing'.

The Exercise of Discretion

The judge really decided at an early stage that since the building was up and done, it was only sensible to leave it.
A barrister reviewing the outcome

Something had obviously gone terribly wrong and Justice O'Bryan was faced with the classic dilemma. The permit was found to be invalid but both the residents and the Wades were held to be innocent of wrongdoing. So who should suffer? Ultimately, the judge was required to 'exercise his discretion'—that is to say, to take all relevant matters into account and make a just and wise decision. The test was based upon the notion that the decision should favour whoever could prove the greater detriment:

The learned trial Judge's task involved doing equity between the parties by making a comparison between the detriment and damage suffered by the residents including any harm to the public resulting from the invalid permit and the extensions illegally made, with the hardship and damage which would be suffered by the Wades if . . . [they were required to demolish].[30]

Justice O'Bryan was anxious to finally resolve the matter and accordingly rejected the argument that a decision should be deferred pending an application for a valid permit. He held that the Wades had proceeded in good faith and that,

> I accept the evidence of Mr Day that the cost of removing the first floor extensions to the Wade house is approximately $35,000. I also accept Mr Neesham's submission that the consequences for the Wades could be disastrous. The consequences of removal of the first floor extension would impose an intolerable financial burden upon the Wades and might be psychologically disturbing to them. I weigh up against the expenses of removal, the fact that the plaintiffs with *locus standi* to sue have proved minimal damage in *money terms*. Accordingly, in the exercise of my discretion I must decline to grant the plaintiffs the injunctive relief claimed.[31] (author's italics)

The point was made by Tim Colebatch in his article in the *Age* that while considerable weight was given to the detriment which might be occasioned to the Wades, there was little evidence of consideration for the suffering of the residents, occasioned by the illegal building, though for the Browns Justice O'Bryan described the extensions as a 'disaster'. Moreover, it was significant that the residents' detriment is dismissed in the context of 'minimal damage in money terms'.

There was conflicting evidence concerning diminution in value caused by the development. Valuers for the residents estimated a total diminution for the properties of approximately $30,000. This was disputed by the Council and the Wades and the judge held that the extent of diminution of value was difficult to assess in the absence of sales experience. The assessment should, strictly speaking, be confined to those residents held to have legal standing. As we shall see, Dr Falk and the Thornes were held not to have standing and if we delete their estimated diminution, we are left with a total of $22,500.

The evidence of detriment to the Wades is highly questionable. No evidence was provided in relation to the 'psychological damage', Norman Day's evidence was not tested, and the detailed evidence provided by the residents' architect obtained at the suggestion of the judge concerning the demolition costs was not even adverted to.

However, a much more important question was not resolved. At what stage is it appropriate to consider detriment to the Wades? Was it at the time of the issue of the writ or shortly thereafter at the injunction hearing when Justice Gobbo said to them that if they proceeded beyond this point, they did so at their own peril? Or should we look at the completed building, as did Justice O'Bryan, on the basis that the Wades are entitled to claim everything completed in the face of Justice Gobbo's (and other) warnings?

Surely there can be no doubt that the correct point in time was, at the latest, that indicated by Justice Gobbo, or earlier, on the basis that the Wades proceeded in the face of many warnings, 'at their own risk'?

At the time of the hearing before Justice Gobbo, as noted in chapter 3, the work undertaken was not substantial and was estimated by a quantity surveyor at $5000–$5700. Obviously, if the trial had been held then, or the injunction hearing proceeded with, then the residents must have won convincingly, since their detriment was certainly found to be 'substantial'.

It is also fascinating to note the extent to which the decision was based upon dollars and cents and we are forcibly reminded of, 'the English law's obsession with money damages . . .'[32] While there will be many cases where it is convenient to quantify detriment in terms of dollars and cents, the *opposite* is normally the case in town planning cases. Indeed, the general principle before the Appeals Board is that financial and economic factors are irrelevant.

The judge seems to give little weight to the very serious loss of amenity to the residents. One is left with the suspicion that since the Supreme Court is rarely concerned with town planning cases, the judge may have been rather more disposed to apply the conventional common law criterion—namely, that of quantifiable damages in dollars and cents. Town planning cases are concerned with grounds which normally preclude consideration of financial criteria unlike, say, a motor car running down case. Established principles of town planning in this case would embrace amenity issues such as loss of sunlight, overlooking, bulk appearance of building, etc.

Remedies and Costs

> We proved that the permit was invalid which was the substance
> of the case. It was a very wrong decision.
>
> *Neil Brown, QC*

No other aspect of the case has caused so much dismay and
controversy as the decision in relation to costs. As we saw,
when considering the exercise of discretion, the judge based
his decision upon the balance of detriment test and concluded
that the Wades would suffer more if they were required to
demolish the offending extension than would the residents if
the extension remained. He therefore refrained, although
ruling that the permit was null and void, from awarding the
injunction sought. The residents had also sought damages but
had played this remedy down since it was not dollars and
cents in any punitive sense that they wanted. Rather they
sought to ensure that the due process of law was observed and
their rights protected.

Despite the fact that the residents were pitted against the
massive resources of the Council, Lloyds of London (the
Council's insurers) and the Wades, they nevertheless established that the Council had been unco-operative, was guilty of
serious maladministration in its planning department and
consequently, that the permit issued was invalid and the
building constructed in the face of litigation and Justice
Gobbo's warnings. The residents had won on what the judge
had described as the 'main issue as to the validity of the permit'
only to find that he then declined to provide any remedy.

The judge ordered the residents to pay all the Wades' costs,
all their own and half those of the Council—in total, approximately $760,000. The residents were devastated. Many lawyers
and observers quite independent of the case have subsequently
expressed astonishment.

The judge handed down his separate judgement concerning
costs on 9 May 1984. He adverted to 'the general rule as to
costs', when, 'In the absence of special circumstances, a successful litigant should receive his costs from the unsuccessful
litigant'.

The disputed first floor extensions photographed from
11 Fitzgibbon Street.

'At that time (issue of the writ) the alterations were complete or,
for practical purposes almost so'. This critical finding of the full
court does not accord with contemporary photographs. . . . .

The shadow cast on a bright sunny day across the Brown's rear garden.

The judge cited the British case of *Ottway v. Jones* (1955) 1 W.L.R. 706, where an unsuccessful plaintiff had had his costs paid for by the defendant because it was shown that the defendant's conduct 'was a serious nuisance or annoyance'. In that case, as in the Wade case, the plaintiffs only failed because discretionary relief was not awarded. Many issues can well be argued but I do not think it could possibly be put that the Council was not guilty of 'nuisance and annoyance' and that if its house had been properly in order, it would never have issued an invalid permit.

The judge could have required the Council to pay the residents' costs, or alternatively, he could have simply required the parties to bear their own costs. In the Ottway case Lord Parker indicated that it would no doubt be rare for a successful defendant to pay the unsuccessful plaintiff's costs and that, 'In general it will be sufficient to deprive the successful defendant of his costs and not to order him to pay the plaintiff's costs'. The judge chose neither of these alternatives in the present case, but required the residents to pay half the Council's costs since although they had succeeded on the 'main issue', 'on all the other issues all of the residents were unsuccessful'.

It should be noted that for the lawyer, a 'successful' litigant is one who wins by obtaining the remedy sought, regardless of whether he has proved the main substance of the case. Thus it seems, the residents were not successful in the judge's eyes, and it was the proven negligent Council and the Wades, who held the invalid permit and who had built illegally at an 'unusually rapid pace', in the face of warnings and litigation, who were deemed the successful parties. *Through the Looking Glass?*

The judge observed that the residents lost on all the other issues. One has the sense that we are concerned with some form of point scoring contest. In any event, the judge is clearly factually mistaken. Apart from the 'main issue' which was won on two bases, many other significant issues were won by the residents, and a number are set out in the next summary section.

It is possible that the judge may have been confused regarding the nature and thrust of the residents' claim against the Council. At the outset, they had wanted to bring the action against both the Council and the Wades, but prior to the commencement of the hearing, Murray, on behalf of the Council, had pleaded with the residents not to join the Council as a defendant. He claimed that this could offend the Commissioners who had declared their intention to commence proceedings to revoke the permit, given co-operation. The residents did co-operate but alas, the permit was not revoked and at the hearing, Murray's barrister, Buckner, then argued that the non-joining of the Council as a defendant in the first instance should be held against the residents!

It is apparent from the costs judgement and from the primary judgement, that the judge took the view that the substance of the action was against the Wades, against whom the injunction was sought, while damages, he said, 'were not sought against the Council . . . The City of Melbourne was joined as party some time after the action commenced to assist the plaintiffs to obtain injunctive relief against the Wades'.[33] A barrister for the residents says this is not correct since they were motivated to join the Council as a defendant, and did so, just as soon as it failed to revoke the permit. The barristers for the residents also deny withdrawal of the claim for damages against the Council. A barrister for the other side says they did. There is no record of such withdrawal on the transcript to my knowledge. This may well explain the judge's reluctance to award any costs against the Council. Putting it simply, 'the action was against the Wades, it failed, so those who brought the action must bear the costs'.

With regard to the Wades, the residents had been 'wholly unsuccessful', and failed against them because they could not prove misrepresentation. 'The principal relief sought by the residents', said the judge, was 'in the form of a mandatory injunction against the Wades . . . The reasons for not granting relief had nothing to do with the conduct of the Council',[34] and therefore the Council ought not to be required to bear the Wades' costs.

Having dealt with the costs of the residents and the Wades, the judge finally turned to those of the Council. He came to the breathtaking conclusion that the Council, 'must also be regarded as a successful defendant, in the sense that the claim brought by the residents against the Council failed altogether'.[35] However, he conceded that, 'The Court found that the Council failed to administer the Act properly, despite assertions to the contrary by the Council. A proportion of the costs of the Council of the trial are clearly attributable to its unsuccessful defence of the allegation that the Council issued an invalid permit . . .', and he accordingly required the Council to pay half its costs and the residents the balance.

As Kim Lockwood reported in the *Herald* on 27 May 1985, the total costs had already mounted to approximately $765,600 which required the four families to come up with $191,400 each! I do not presume to dispute the judge's formulation of the law, but one cannot help but wonder at the manner in which he exercised his discretion. The litigation had sprung from the proven errors and omissions of the Council, the residents had won convincingly on the 'main issue' and other issues against enormous resources; to suggest that they should additionally win on a range of other issues seems rather mean. But then, perhaps, that is an inevitable fault of our adversarial legal system. 'I went in to win', said Ian Murray, looking back on the case. Many lawyers would think that to be perfectly proper, but do such attitudes enable the relevant parties to focus upon the main issues in the community interest? The residents were the 'opposition' as Murray put it to me, but they are ratepayers like anyone else and the Council has fiduciary and other responsibilities towards them in the interests of running a decent city.

In any event, the ruling by the judge remains an enigma. The residents' counsel were astonished with the result, having held the view that even given that they lost on the issue of misrepresentation, they could not possibly be required to pay any portion of the Council's costs. Even Murray for the Council felt that the residents could well succeed on the issue of costs against the Council and he remarked to a barrister prior to judgement, 'we are here to collect our medicine'.

Summary

Serves 'em right!

Doug Wade[36]

The outcome for the Wades could doubtless be viewed by some as a triumph for the 'individual' seeking to get on with his own business free from interfering 'busybodies'. Comments by Wade to the media indicate that he felt that the residents got what they deserved.

For the residents, the litigation was a catastrophe. There are also additional important consequences. First, it is now very doubtful what remedy, if any, is available to residents who, seeking to uphold the public law, suffer substantial detriment as a consequence of an invalid permit being issued and who are unable to convince an erring Council to revoke the permit. Extraordinarily, it seems that the holder of such a permit should, like the Wades, belt on with the work at full speed to ensure that he can prove maximum detriment should that be necessary.

The lack of an appropriate prescribed remedy then was at the heart of the problem. Resort to the Supreme Court with its delays and expense created more problems than it solved. It was too slow, too costly and quite unable to expedite the matter. With the benefit of hindsight, once litigation had commenced, given the protracted delays, the succession of seven barristers for the residents, the lack of adequate court recording facilities before Justice Gobbo, the range of complex issues flowing from inadequate ordinances, the unco-operative Commissioners, Council staff, legal advisers and indemnifying insurance company and given the death of a prime witness, it is not difficult to foresee problems for the residents.

We can also see how, given the test of *detriment* applied by the judge, it became important for the Wades to advance their position through completion of the work without a valid permit. The Appeals Board and Justice Gobbo shrank from such a principle and the latter made it crystal clear that further building would be at the risk of the Wades. Alas, he was wrong; *they* were not prejudiced by their continued building, it proved their salvation! Given the extensive court delays and other difficulties, some of the critical issues became muddied and do not seem to have been forcefully put to Justice O'Bryan.

We may also ask why, following the death of Chisholm, the residents' lawyers did not resolve the admissability of her evidence, having regard to the fact that their failure to prove misrepresentation could have serious implications concerning costs. It developed into an emotive and critical issue, was not proved and was the one issue which, having failed, rebounded upon the residents. They lost on other issues but their position concerning those was always cogent, reasonable and defensible.

Many questions remain unanswered—for example, why didn't Justice O'Bryan and the lawyers look a little more deeply into what occurred before Justice Gobbo? Why did Justice O'Bryan so quickly conclude that the detriment for the Wades would outweigh that occasioned to the residents? Their loss of amenity has been substantial and the crippling legal costs will now force them to sell their homes unless a last minute 'act of mercy' is forthcoming. No real reference to these dire consequences appears to have attended the judge's considerations to our knowledge. And how was he so comfortable about ignoring the illegality, the inherent wisdom in the notion that the public law should be upheld and that public bodies should be accountable for their wrongful decisions?

Summary of Findings

1. It was held that John Noonan took account of or placed too much emphasis upon the consents given by Miss Chisholm and Notini so as to cause him to err in forming an opinion pursuant to s. 18B of the Planning Act that the grant of the permit may not cause substantial detriment to persons other than the applicant. The residents succeeded on this issue and the permit was accordingly held to be null and void.

2. It was held that no responsible authority (Council) could have formed the opinion for the purposes of s. 18B that the grant of a permit may not have caused substantial detriment to any person other than the applicant. The residents also succeeded on this (the 'main issue' concerning the invalidity of the permit), and again, the permit was held to be invalid.

3. On the relatively minor issue as to whether the permit was invalid because the Council acted beyond its powers by delegating authority to D. Goodwin, the residents succeeded in proving that the Council had acted beyond its powers. However, the judge did not invalidate the permit on this basis since the irregularity was unsubstantial. Thus although the Council had acted wrongly, the finding was against the residents.

4. It was held that no permit was required under the Melbourne Metropolitan Planning Scheme for the proposed extensions. To reach this conclusion, it was necessary to include within the calculations a number of shanty structures at the rear. The judge described the Scheme as 'confusing, contradictory . . . a nightmare to administer and a paradise for lawyers', and the evidence concerning whether or not there had been an increase, served 'to show the absurdity of the whole exercise'.

It was within that context that the residents failed to win this leg of the case although it could be said that the issue was by now only of academic interest. In passing, one might observe that the issue would never have been litigated if the Government had amended the Scheme adequately, or if the Council had done as their consultant said they should and processed the application for a planning scheme permit in the first instance.

5. The Wades were exonerated from the claim that they had perpetrated false representations, mis-statements and omissions to obtain the consents of adjoining owners in order to cause the Council to grant an invalid permit. The residents lost this issue convincingly. With hindsight, their advisers should have thoroughly reviewed the position and therefore probably have dropped the claims altogether following the death of their prime witness Miss Chisholm, which obviously raised major problems concerning the admissability of her affidavits.

6. The judge was not persuaded that Day concealed material facts or made false representations to the Council which may have caused the Council to grant an invalid permit and even if Day were guilty of deception this did not implicate the Wades.

Again, the residents failed on this issue, although along the way they established the inadequacy of the Council's procedures and that the administration itself from the most senior level had been unco-operative. Given appropriate procedures and evaluation, the Council would never have issued the invalid permit.

7. The claims by the Wades and the Council that the residents did not have the requisite standing to bring the action failed. The judge clarified the law by adopting a narrow common

law definition, but even so most of the residents, and certainly the critical ones, succeeded in establishing standing. It is not significant, in this context, that Dr Falk and the Thornes were not given standing.

Of the significant issues identified by the judge, the residents won three of them convincingly including the main issue. However, they lost convincingly both the issues of misrepresentation and deception. They also lost the issues concerning the planning scheme and the delegation of authority although these were by then academic. The former had arisen due to the Government's drafting inadequacies, inadequate Council procedures and the failure of the Council to require an application to be processed, while the latter arose due to an action by the Council which was not lawful.

Some Ancillary Issues Won by the Residents

The residents succeeded in:
• Establishing substantial detriment contrary to the claims of the Council and the Wades.
• Establishing (contrary to the Wades' assertions), that the wall shared with the Browns and demolished by the Wades was in fact a party wall. This was important because it proved the Wade house was defined as a 'row house' and therefore fell within the ambit of the Planning Scheme.
• Resisting the contention that they were stopped from bringing the proceedings, or bound by laches or otherwise barred.
• In resisting the contention that they were bound by the revocation proceedings.
• Establishing serious maladministration at the Council level.

It is within this context that the judge exercised his discretion in favour of the Wades due to the potential detriment that demolition would involve. He declined to grant a remedy for the residents although the permit was invalid and the extensions illegal. Since no remedies were awarded, the residents were 'unsuccessful' and therefore must bear the brunt of the costs since, he said, there were not 'special circumstances' in this case which would be required to determine otherwise.

Judicial Decision Making

This chapter commenced with Justice O'Bryan's proposition that essentially the issues were legal and must be resolved without regard to social, political or personal considerations. Would that such cases could be resolved within a vacuum consisting of some form of quintessential justice. No doubt some people naïvely imagine that that is how decisions are made but quite obviously, in the real world, this is not so. It is inevitable that personal value judgements and the whole armoury of our accumulated knowledge and experience will be brought to bear by whomsoever is involved—be he a judge, a witness or the court cleaner. Are we to believe that the judge exercises his discretion free of personal value judgements?

How do judges make decisions and why were Justice O'Bryan's findings in stark contrast to those of the Chairman of the Appeals Board? It seems that the judge accepted the Neesham thesis that the Wades landed innocently in South Parkville to receive an unwarranted hostile response. I believe this to be unfair and that generally Australians respond warmly to newcomers provided they are reasonably friendly and open in turn.

Justice O'Bryan has had very little background or experience in the town planning jurisdiction which must take account of amenity considerations and community aspirations which have no place in the traditional legal vocabulary. Although he would like to believe that the issues were essentially legal, in the final analysis, the decision involved other grounds according to other values.

From an early point in the judgement Justice O'Bryan expressed either direct or indirect disapproval of the residents. For them to try and protect their homes from the illegal construction was a 'remarkable crusade of action, leading . . . [to] this lengthy and expensive hearing'. He is clearly mystified by their approach:

> . . . on 28th May, workmen began to demolish the second storey wing walls and balcony at the front of the Wade house, to the dismay of a number of persons in the neighbourhood, including the residents, Thorne, Forsey and Brown. By the following day, their dismay had *turned to anger* and when Mr and Mrs Wade

arrived outside the house to inspect the works, *a hostile crowd* gathered . . .

Mrs Wade and her young children were frightened by the *hostile crowd* and Mr and Mrs Wade were affronted . . . they became soured by what they regarded as an *aggressive and intolerable intrusion* into their private affairs from a group of strangers who had chosen to enlist both media and political influence to serve their ends. I believe that Mr and Mrs Wade are not insensitive people but when they received a *hostile*, *unfriendly welcome*, they were forced to adopt an uncompromising attitude to defend their concept.[37] (author's italics)

We gain the clear impression that the judge, like Joh Bjelke-Petersen, believes there is something wrong with people gathering together and contacting the media and the relevant responsible politicians in order to try and resolve a public issue. The conclusions drawn by the judge concerning the residents' attitudes are not supported by the views of independent witnesses who unfortunately had no opportunity to rebut the evidence given by the Wades. Most of the plaintiff residents, like Brown, were not even present on 28 May! Dr Falk knew nothing of the matter at that stage. I was present when the television crews were filming the workmen. The Wades were clearly racing against time to get the work done at the front prior to their meeting at the Town Hall (and potential prosecution). It was obviously very embarrassing for them and they literally fled from the media.

At no stage over the past four years has the media, or anyone else who might be regarded as reasonably independent, been foolish enough to suggest that the Wades had been met with 'hostility' or that residents had made an 'intolerable intrusion into their private affairs'. My own reaction, having been present at dozens of similar gatherings, was merely that the Wades had been publicly exposed as they should have been, and that this was all good honest fun—all in the day's work. The 'frightened' children I observed, waved to us from the upstairs balcony.

The judgement contains other examples of Justice O'Bryan's personal views about the residents. Thus he refers to the residents going to, 'extraordinary lengths to protect the streetscape', and although 'each witness called impressed me as an honest witness he prefers Wade's evidence to Notini's concerning misrepresentation and with regard to Miss Chisholm felt that she may have been influenced in forming her opinions by other neighbours. Justice O'Bryan concluded that in obtaining the consent signatures Wade 'had no motive to deceive or conceal anything from Miss Chisholm or any other person'. Now we know that Wade was anxious to get on with the work, that Day had told him that the consents would speed the process up and that elevations and a model could have been produced if Wade and Day had chosen to make them available. Of course Wade had a motive. But the judge said he was, 'impressed by Wade's demeanour in the witness box. Mr Wade gave his evidence quietly . . .'

Ultimately after ninety pages of rigorous legal elaboration the judge had to exercise his discretion almost entirely upon non-legal grounds. He then agreed in one crucial paragraph that the Wades would suffer 'psychological damage', and adopted Day's untested assertion regarding the cost of demolition. The detriment to the residents was casually dismissed as 'minimal damage in money terms'.

Footnotes

[1] Judgement of Justice O'Bryan (Supreme Court of Victoria), *P. Thorne (and Others) v. D. and R. Wade, Councillors and Citizens of the City of Melbourne*, p. 11a.

[2] Michael Kirby, *Reform the Law*, OUP, Melbourne, 1983, pp. 169, 254.

[3] Transcript of the hearing of the Supreme Court before Justice O'Bryan, p. 1794.

[4] Judgement of Justice O'Bryan, *op. cit.*, p. 81a.

[5] *Ibid*, p. 36a.

[6] *Ibid*, p. 78a.

[7] *Ibid*, pp. 79a, 80a.

[8] Transcript of the Supreme Court, *op. cit.*, p. 2844.

[9] Judgement of Justice O'Bryan, *op. cit.*, p. 88a.

[10] Transcript of the Supreme Court, *op. cit.*, p. 2450.

[11] *Ibid*, p. 869.

[12] Judgement of Justice O'Bryan, *op. cit.*, p. 35a.

[13] *Ibid*, p. 89a.

[14] *Ibid*, p. 90a.

[15] *Ibid*, p. 56a.

[16] *Ibid*, p. 51a.

[17] *Ibid*, p. 56a.

[18] *Ibid*, p. 45a.

[19] *Ibid*, p. 65a.

[20] *Ibid*, p. 58a.

[21] The first quote is from Sid Forsey, 'Transcription of Notes Made at Injunction Attempt before Justice Gobbo'. The second quote is from the judgement of Justice O'Bryan, *op. cit.*, p. 93a.

[22] Full Court of Appeal judgement (Marks, McGarvie and Kaye JJ), p. 38.

[23] Miles Lewis in conversation with the author, mid-October 1985. The rest of the quote deleted due to defamation laws.

[24] Judgement of Justice O'Bryan, *op. cit.*, p. 29a.

[25] Transcript of the Supreme Court, *op. cit.*, p. 869.

[26] Trevor Huggard, who was engaged as engineering consultant, soon found 'difficulty with the plans and asked Day to clarify them. Day visited Huggard's offices in North Carlton and Huggard asked him what extensions were proposed at the rear. Day's alleged reply cannot be disclosed due to defamatiion laws.

[27] Letter from Miles Lewis to the Town Clerk, 4 October 1982.

[28] *Ibid*.

[29] *Ibid*.

[30] Full Court of Appeal judgement, *op. cit.*, p. 39.

[31] Judgement of Justice O'Bryan, *op. cit.*, p. 95a.

[32] Kirby, *op. cit.*, p. 181.

[33] Judgement of Justice O'Bryan on costs, p. 3701.

[34] *Ibid*, p. 3701.

[35] *Ibid*, p. 3699.

[36] The *Sunday Press*, 22 April 1984.

[37] Judgement of Justice O'Bryan, *op. cit.*, p. 39a.

5

Appeal to the Full Court of the Supreme Court

The law is not for ordinary people who live in Parkville.

Crispin Hull[1]

The judgement of Justice O'Bryan had generated widespread dismay. It was not to become a *cause célèbre* until after the Full Court hearing but it had certainly become a public issue. In a major feature article in the *Age* on 9 February 1985, Roy Eccleston endeavoured to outline the history of the conflict. Unfortunately, he sought to cover both the Appeals Board and Supreme Court hearings and many readers were confused by the problems at the front of the house in contrast to those at the rear. It was headed THE HOUSE THAT DOUG BOUGHT and it was soon followed by a stinging article in the *Melbourne Times*, THE PUP THAT DOUG BOUGHT by Keith Cornish. This article attacked both Government and Council for their failure to accept responsibility and claimed, 'This saga represents a tedious recital of bureaucratic intransigence, incompetence and moral cowardice'. A spate of letters appeared in the press including the well reasoned statement of solicitor Kevin Zervos who pointed out that the decision, 'could act as a very real deterrent to those ordinary citizens that seek to uphold community standards'.[2]

The residents were in a state of temporary shock. Their

attitude might best be described in the words of Ken Brown, who it will be recalled was most affected by the extensions. In a letter to the *Melbourne Times* on 10 July 1985 Brown made his feelings plain:

PROTECTING THE INNOCENT

In June 1982 I became aware that my neighbour had obtained a planning permit to extend his house, and that his proposed extensions would seriously affect my property.

I spoke to the council planning officer concerned, who clearly had no idea what he had permitted but was prepared to defend his decision no matter how outrageous.

In the absence of elected councillors I spoke to the Chief Commissioner, who told me that he had put the whole matter into the hands of the Town Clerk.

The Town Clerk, however, refused to see me, or even to answer my letters. I resorted to legal action and, with others, sought to have construction stopped, but the Supreme Court judge refused even to hear the application because it would take too long. Instead he declared the matter urgent.

My lawyers protested that this would allow building to continue and would prejudice my case because the court would be unwilling to order demolition of a completed building, but the judge said no — if the permit is invalid then whether the building is finished or not would not affect the outcome.

The neighbours, well aware of my complaints and contention that their permit was invalid, built their extension. They had plenty of time to do so because the urgent hearing did not eventuate for more than a year.

When it was heard the judge decided, that the permit was indeed invalid, and that the extensions to the house were a 'disaster' for me and had caused 'damage' to my house. However, he was not willing to do anything about that because of the effects that removal of the extensions might have on the owners — a reason which contrasts sharply with the statements of the judge at the previous hearing. I must pay my share of the ruinous court costs.

My mistake, of course, was to think that the law protected the weak and innocent — it does not. On this occasion it has protected the reponsible authority which refused to admit its error, and hid behind its giant insurance company.

The whole affair is utterly ridiculous, but the real question is, what are you going to do if you find that your neighbour has a planning permit, issued wrongly by the local council, for works

which you believe will be disastrous for you and damaging to
your home?

K. C. Brown
Fitzgibbon Street
Parkville

The residents went to their lawyers who sought an opinion
from their barrister. Neil Brown, QC, who had been horrified
by the decision, was no longer available but Garde was now
joined by Brian Shaw, QC—one of the most respected minds
at the Victorian bar. Although his field is normally commercial
law, where he frequently handles major corporate disputes,
he quickly turned his mind to the central theme when he
joined with Garde to give an opinion to the residents
regarding grounds for an appeal:

> In all the circumstances, we consider that there are reasonable
> prospects . . . although it must be borne in mind, as we have
> already pointed out, that it is difficult to upset a judgement as to
> discretionary matters . . . It may be thought extraordinary that
> the residents failed although they successfully established that
> the permit granted to the Wades was invalid; that the Council
> had acted unlawfully in breach of the public law; that the
> residents had commenced proceedings promptly; that some of
> the residents had standing to bring the proceedings; that the
> residents had suffered detriment, loss of amenity, and damage
> [meaning monetary loss], albeit minimal, and had been deprived
> of the legal right to object to the proposed works; and that the
> works were substantially performed after a summons seeking an
> interlocutory injunction restraining the Wades from proceeding
> with the works had been issued and brought on before Gobbo J.
> in the Practice Court.

The reader may wonder that the residents could contemplate
an appeal. In the first place, they believed they had suffered
a fundamental injustice and there were many independent
lawyers who shared that view. Secondly, and most importantly,
if they did not appeal, then they were faced with the huge
costs order against them with no right of relief. Thirdly, it
was put to them that they had quite a good case and that this
should assist them in negotiations and could only improve
their position, since they couldn't possibly do any worse!
They also managed to obtain some legal aid. The Wades may
have also obtained legal aid but this has not been confirmed.

Certainly, the residents were hopeful that while the case remained active, they retained some hope that a settlement might be achieved, particularly in the light of the considerable criticism that Justice O'Bryan had directed at the Council—and the fact that the Council itself had become increasingly sympathetic to their position.

On 19 April 1984 the residents lodged their appeal to the Full Court of the Supreme Court. For some time, everyone's attention was then diverted to the Appeals Board hearing which was sandwiched between the two Supreme Court hearings. It came on, as we have seen, on 1 May and the determination was delivered on 27 July. On that same day, the Council deputation of Councillors Peter Black and Tom Lynch, Bethke and Murray, met with the Council's insurers, Lloyds of London, in London. As we have learned, the party returned with absolutely nothing tangible for their efforts.

On the other hand, the Council continued its efforts to persuade the Government to help resolve the matter. On 28 August 1984, a Council deputation including Murray presented a submission to the Minister for Local Government in which it stated:

> The Council is faced with a difficult and worrying problem which it is unable to resolve and believes that solution may only be achievable through State Government intervention. The Council believes that injustice may be done to the residents involved . . . In short what broadly occurred was that the Council permitted a second storey row house extension to take place without giving affected neighbours the opportunity to object or appeal and thereby those neighbours lost their statutory rights.

The Council was seeking financial input from the Government on the basis that the error could have occurred with any council in Victoria and that subsequent to the case, councils now understand their obligations to advertise and that accordingly, the problem would not be a precedent. Again, on 19 December, Bethke and Murray met with Evan Walker, Minister for Planning and Environment, to seek special legislation from the Government.

It was not until March 1985 that Simmonds, the Minister for Local Government, wrote to the Council advising that both he and Walker had concluded that they did not believe it was appropriate to assist with special legislation.

Once again negotiations did not bear fruit and on 7 March the Full Court appeal commenced before Justices Kaye, McGarvie and Marks. After some 9½ sitting days it finished on 26 March, when the Court reserved its decision.

Judgement Day

For judgement of the Full Court of the Supreme Court. Banco Court 10 a.m. 21 May 1985.

I will not forget that bleak wintry morning when I entered the Banco Court to find myself transported back in time. It is a high ceilinged chamber in the best Victorian tradition — plenty of dark timber pannelling and the judges bench set up high above us lesser mortals. Why Banco, I reflected; doubtless the answer is buried in musty legal calendars. The judge's associate was flustering with papers, pretending to be busy. The barristers and solicitors came swinging in, bewigged and costumed, smiling and joking to one another — lounging on their leather upholstered benches. Residents and friends came in gingerly, trying to hide their misery and appear comfortable. Doug Wade sat by himself behind his lawyers with his customary impassive expression. Some Councillors arrived, namely Trevor Huggard, Lorna Rolfe, Gordon Moffat and Tom Lynch. Several journalists drifted into the press box.

I cannot think of those courts, but I think of Charles Dickens' *Bleak House* and the case of *Jarndyce v. Jarndyce* . . .

> This is the Court of Chancery; which has its decaying houses and its blighted lands in every shire . . . *which gives to monied might the means abundantly of wearying out the right* . . . the Lord Chancellor . . . with a foggy glory round his head, softly fenced in with crimson cloth and curtains, addressed by a large advocate with great whiskers, a little voice, and an interminable brief, and outwardly directing his contemplation to the lantern in the roof, where he can see nothing but fog . . . *Jarndyce and Jarndyce* drones on . . . (author's italics)

My reverie was shattered by the judges' door being thrown open to admit all three judges and the Associate commanded us to rise. The three strode quickly to their seats. Gone were the amiable relaxed men who had sat through days of learned legal debate; smiling, lounging and browsing their way through arguments, jokes, half-jokes and non-jokes from ingratiating barristers. From their Olympian perspective, they stared down, avoiding all eye contact, their blank bewigged faces seemingly prepared to pronounce the death penalty, as indeed they might—having assumed an ashen mask-like quality, as if whitened by powders, deemed appropriate for their 18th-century bewigged coiffures.

Mr Justice Kaye quickly read the verdict. The residents' grounds of appeal had all failed, both in relation to remedies and costs. The judges thereupon quickly rose and departed, wigs, gowns and prestige intact and swirling about. I remember sitting stunned, desperately trying to absorb it . . . as if in a terrific car accident . . . the sense that time was ticking by and that people were moving about . . . but unable to comprehend.

The residents had appealed on 37 grounds which may be summarised:

1. That the judge, having found the permit to be null and void, should have provided the residents with a remedy and awarded costs in their favour.
2. The alterations and additions constituted 'new building' and accordingly the Wades should have been required to apply for a planning scheme permit.
3. The Thornes and Dr Falk should have been awarded standing.

We will not deal with the appeal in detail but certain findings of the judges can be noted at the outset which may serve to place their views in context.

First, the issue before the judges was not whether or not Justice O'Bryan had been right or wrong. They were not asked to consider how they would have decided the case if they had been in his shoes. They were rather, required to consider whether he had been 'unreasonable or plainly unjust', or acted upon 'a wrong principle, if he allows extraneous or irrelevant matters to guide or affect him, mistakes the facts . . .'[3] One need hardly point out that the residents were accordingly faced with an even higher burden of proof than encountered previously. They were now required, after an extensive hearing, to review the performance of their colleague. In a sense, Justice O'Bryan was now on trial by his peers.

The Full Court judgement seeks to confine itself scrupulously to legal issues. Only very occasionally do the judges disclose their personal views with the occasional reference to 'uncompromising' residents and their acceptance of the Wade/Neesham thesis that, 'The degree of hostility with which the crowd expressed its protests was such that Mrs Wade and her children became afraid for their safety'. The judges carefully avoid the slightest possible suggestion that at any stage Wade or Day had acted less than perfectly. Constantly, the onus is placed upon the residents to establish that there was evidence that Justice O'Bryan 'was in error', had been 'unreasonable or plainly unjust', and again, 'In our opinion, it was not shown that in the exercise of his discretion to withhold relief His Honour took into account unauthorised considerations or omitted to take into account considerations which he ought to have'.

Second, having outlined the burden of proof that confronted the residents, the judges then stated in a crucial passage that:

> *The principal challenge to the legality of the permit was founded on allegations that it was issued upon consents of Miss Chisholm and Mr Notini which had been procured by false representations or misrepresentations made to them by Mr Wade.* Nevertheless, His Honour totally rejected the residents' allegations that the consents of Miss Chisholm and Mr Notini resulted from false representations or misrepresentations made by Mr Wade. His Honour's finding vindicated Mr Wade's belief at the time of the issue of the writ that he had not falsely represented the plan to Mr Notini and Miss Chisholm. *In addition at that time the alterations were completed or, for practical purposes, almost so.*
>
> In those circumstances, it would not have been open to His Honour to conclude that the Wades, by continuing and completing the work, had sought to achieve a *fait accompli* for the purpose of strengthening their position at the trial of the action. There is no similarity between the conduct of the Wades and that of the defendant in *Day v. Pingten*.[4] (author's italics in paragraph 1)

The above findings which I have italicised are plainly in error. The principal challenge to the validity of the permit was not based upon false representations as has been pointed out. It is the prerogative of the plaintiff to set out what is fundamental to his case. Neil Brown did not even mention the issue of false representation when he summarised the substance of his case during his opening. Certainly, Justice O'Bryan made no such finding as we have seen.[5]

Further, as pointed out, there is no basis upon which it could be concluded that at the time of the issue of the writ the building was complete, or almost so—even given the capacity of the Wades to build as rapidly as they did! Justice O'Bryan made no such finding although in his detailed history of the matter he does record, that 15 months after the issue of the writ, 'The building works, other than the proposal at the front have now been completed'. How then, did the judges come to such conclusions? One must assume that these findings, which are fundamental to the ultimate decisions, say much for the skill of the Wades' barrister Neesham who repeatedly claimed that the building was all but complete and repeatedly raised the issue of misrepresentation in a successful endeavour to denigrate the residents. Certainly none of the barristers have been able to satisfactorily explain the findings to me. It is fair to say that both residents and barristers were bewildered.

The judgement then seeks to contrast the actions of the Wades and the defendants in the *Day v. Pinglen* case: 'By contrast, the Wades, in the belief that they had not by deception procured the permit and with reason for believing that the permit was a valid one, completed the work either immediately before or shortly after the issue of the writ'.[6]

It is in that extraordinary context that the decision was reached. Let us now briefly summarise the findings of the Full Court.

Summary of Findings

1. Standing

It will be recalled that the residents, save for the Thornes and Dr Falk, had succeeded in establishing standing before Justice O'Bryan. Although not a major appeal issue, it was raised again on the basis that if the judge were wrong, then he necessarily excluded a relevant consideration when he exercised his discretion. The judgement points out that standing could derive either from infringement of a private right or, 'secondly, where no private right is interfered with but the plaintiff, in respect of his public right, suffers special damage peculiar to himself from the interference with the public right'.[7]

With regard to the second leg, it was held that the three residents had failed to establish 'detriment consonent with the concept of "damage peculiar" to themselves, that is . . . above that of the ordinary members of the public'.

With regard to the first leg, the judges held that s. 18B does not confer private rights, that the provisions of the Act are administrative in character and are merely intended to make provision for individuals to object in certain circumstances, but that such provisions do not thereby create private rights. The judges, in holding that the Act provides no private rights, overruled some earlier judical statements and sided with an alternative line of conservative legal statements.

2. Damages

There had been confusion as to whether the residents had abandoned their claim for damages at the previous hearing despite the fact that it was clearly sought as an alternative remedy in the statement of claim.

The judges held that since the residents did not have any private rights conferred by the Act, then a claim for damages could not succeed save through a common law suit such as negligence or nuisance. However, advice from senior counsel had ruled out any serious prospect of a negligence action succeeding as we have seen. In fact, the Full Court said that such an action for damages was never available.

3. Melbourne and Metropolitan Planning Scheme

The residents had pointed out that Justice O'Bryan had not dealt with the lengthily argued issue of whether the extensions constituted 'new building'. The judges agreed that on any view the legislation was ambiguous. They resolved the semantic issue by holding, to the surprise of many lawyers, that the expression, 'new building' is applicable to building which has the effect of increasing floor area. It therefore followed that no permit was required. It also follows that it is not clear what meaning, if any, is added by the words, 'new building' and consequently, an amendment to the planning scheme has been recommended.

4. Denial of Remedies

It was argued by the residents that the judge, in exercising his discretion, should have provided remedies for the residents. The judges replied to this by saying that they had no doubt that 'His Honour was ever-mindful that the alterations and additions to the Wade house were carried out contrary to law . . .[that the permit was] illegally issued', and they then went on to make the findings set out at the beginning of this section, which appear to be plainly in error.

The judges then conclude that Justice O'Bryan was 'mindful' of the substantial detriment which the residents had suffered but that on balance, the detriment to be suffered by the Wades through demolition would be greater than that sustained by the residents through the building remaining complete.

Shaw had adverted to the inadequacy of the evidence regarding the cost of demolition and the total lack of evidence concerning the consequent 'psychological damage'. The judges concluded that the term 'psychological' was not used in a technical sense but was a mere 'figure of speech'.

5. Costs

The judges stated that pursuant of s. 39 of the Supreme Court Act, they had no jurisdiction to hear the appeal as to costs because the section required leave of the trial judge, Justice O'Bryan, and this had not been sought. Counsel for the residents had formed the view that it was unlikely that leave to appeal on the issue of costs would be granted, but neverthe-less believed that if they could win on the merits then costs would 'follow the event'. As we have seen, the residents did not win any of the substantive grounds of appeal.

The judges went further and said that even if the order for costs were reviewable without leave of the trial judge, they did not think that Justice O'Bryan had shown, 'reviewable error in the exercise of his discretion'. They concluded that it would be quite unfair to have expected the City of Melbourne to have paid the costs of the Wades. They pointed out that the allegations against the Wades had included 'fraudulent misrepresentation', that those allegations failed and that the 'courts have long so viewed the seriousness of allegations of dishonesty as to compel an unsuccessful plaintiff making the same to pay the costs of the defendant against whom the allegations are made . . .'[8]

Three comments could be made. First, the judges cited another criterion for awarding costs, namely the extent to which the litigation was consequential upon actions of the 'successful' defendant who, 'has so conducted himself as to lead the plaintiff reasonably to believe that he had a good cause of action against the defendant, and so induce him to bring the action'.[9] The present case surely represents an excellent example of the applicability of this rule whereby the invalid permit issued by the Council through its own ineptitude was the very root of the problem.

Secondly, we observe for the first time the use of the emotive term, 'fraudulent misrepresentation'. It is a term which has not been encountered before in any of the material I have seen. It was certainly not used by the residents nor by Justice O'Bryan. The Full Court clearly placed considerable weight upon 'fraud' which they say was the basis of the residents' case whereas Justice O'Bryan was more concerned with which parties had been successful. It is a vital shift of emphasis.

Thirdly, some time is devoted to the question of who should pay the Wades' costs but there is no reference to who should pay those of the Council. This is indeed puzzling since this was clearly the most controversial aspect of the costs judgement. Can we really be satisfied with the sweeping conclusion, 'In our view, His Honour took into account all matters which were relevant to the question of costs . . .'

These findings, however, are subordinate to the major issues, and it is on those issues, as we have seen, that it is difficult to sustain real confidence.

Footnotes
[1] The *Canberra Times*, 2 June 1985.
[2] The *Age*, 10 April 1984.

[3] Full Court of Appeal judgement (Marks, McGarvie and Kaye JJ), p. 35.

[4] *Ibid.*

[5] See discussion above on the 'main issue' and also Judgement of Justice O'Bryan, (Supreme Court of Victoria), *P. Thorne (and Others) v. D. and R. Wade, Councillors and Citizens of The City of Melbourne*, p. 66a and pp. 13a–19a, where he indicates that his representation is but a subsidiary leg to the second 'main issue'.

[6] Full Court of Appeal judgement, *op. cit.*, p. 38.

[7] *Ibid*, p. 17.

[8] *Ibid*, p. 49.

[9] *Ibid*, p. 46.

6
The Aftermath

Some of us are not quite psychologically buggered yet.

Dr Barbara Falk

I remember coming out of the Banco Court after judgement
had been delivered. Ian Murray for the Council went by with
a grin, 'I told you what would happen', he said. A dejected
knot gathered outside. 'Well', said Trevor Huggard, eventually, 'we can't just give up, we must keep fighting for a
reasonable settlement'. We decided to meet that evening at his
office.

I drove Peter Thorne and Barbara Falk back to her home
where she poured a handsome warming Scotch. Copies of the
judgement arrived but we couldn't really begin to absorb it
yet. Peter Thorne had the wretched task of ringing other
residents and his wife. They seemed to have braced themselves
for the worst. 'Well', Peter finally said, 'it is a complete disaster
and I suppose the good thing about that is, it might sustain
everyone's sense of moral outrage. If the judges had been
reasonable and relieved us of the Council's costs, that might
have been seen by some as a sensible compromise'. I marvelled
at his lateral thinking under such adversity.

That evening Huggard proved a generous host. There
were about fourteen of us, including Councillors. Tom Lynch

gave a lengthy peroration about how it was vital to get the ward Councillors on side as the first step and then talked about the prospects of an appeal to the High Court. I looked wearily at Peter Thorne and Ken Brown and eventually turned to Lynch and said firmly, 'The truth of the matter is that the residents are psychologically buggered'. There was a pregnant silence. Barbara Falk went on carefully writing on a huge writing pad, finished her sentence, placed a full stop at the end with great deliberation and then slowly turned to me reprovingly, 'some of us are not quite psychologically buggered yet'.

After the initial tense moment of embarrassment, we laughed to hear this 74-year-old lady's courageous determination to fight on for justice, regardless of the consequences. The tension had been broken because of her superior moral strength. She was still in there fighting . . . regardless of other lesser mortals.

From that moment, we became more cohesive and focussed upon the need for positive action. We needed to start some sort of a new independent body which would take the pressure off the 'Fitzgibbon Street lot'. They were clearly demoralised —with the exception of Dr Falk.

We needed help. Someone suggested solicitor John Howie because of his ALP contacts and interest in human rights and legal issues. When I explained to him that we were planning to convene a meeting with a targeted audience to try and develop support and a general 'groundswell', he was supportive. Someone then suggested John Power, Professor of Political Science at Melbourne University. I spoke to him and he agreed to be involved and to chair the meeting.

Planning for the meeting proceeded satisfactorily but we soon received news to the effect that the Minister, Evan Walker, was not interested in discussing the plight of the Fitzgibbon Street residents, though he was prepared to discuss the longer term problems of amendments to the Act which would prevent such cases arising again.

The Meeting 13 June 1985

We convened the meeting at Clunies Ross House. The urbane John Power had been a good choice for Chairman. There were 105 people present which was good, considering it was by invitation and had not been advertised. The most pleasing aspect was the number of concerned and influential people present from a wide cross-section of the community. Clearly if we were to get anywhere, we would need all the support we could get. Those present ranged from the Lord Mayor, Eddie Beacham, to former Chancellor of the University, Professor George Weickardt, through to Alan Hunt, the competent shadow Minister for Planning. Overall it went well. The motions passed were:

1. This meeting calls upon the State Government to review the Town and Country Planning Act, in order to ensure that the category of persons entitled to object under the Act is broadly defined in accordance with planning principles rather than the narrower common law test of standing. Such a review is necessary so that responsible authorities will continue to recognise the community's right to object and to participate in the planning processes.

2. This meeting calls upon the State Government to consider broadening the category of persons who may seek redress in the courts so as to avoid the narrow common law rules of standing. As a precedent, s. 123 of the NSW Environmental Planning and Assessment Act, 1979, should be considered, viz.,

> Any persons may bring proceedings in the court for an order to remedy or restrain a breach of this Act, whether or not any right of that person has been or may be infringed by or as a consequence of that breach.

3. This meeting calls upon the State Government to consider amending the Town and Country Planning Act, to provide a quick and easy procedure to oversee technical planning issues such as the validity of permits and the rights of persons to object to applications.

4. That this meeting calls upon the State Government and the Melbourne City Council to accept responsibility to compensate the parties to the Parkville case. If need be, the State Government should provide the legal power for such compensation to be paid.

5. That a body be established, comprised initially of volunteers with the objective of promoting and developing the principles resolved at this meeting.

6. That this meeting sees the Parkville case as an apparent failure in the legal process to administer common justice.

As a consequence of the meeting, the Democracy in Planning Group was formed with Power as Chairman.

Next morning there was a headline in the *Age*, WALKER REJECTS $500,000 WADE CASE BILL. The amount was an underestimate since it was generally believed the total would exceed $600,000. At the meeting, Mr Boyce Pizzey, on behalf of the Minister had said that the Government had no intention of meeting the costs since it did not accept responsibility and did not see itself as being at fault in any way.

There were two speakers. Simon Molesworth, in his capacity as the Deputy Chairman of the National Trust, addressed the legal/planning issues and some of his recommendations were incorporated in the above motions. I accepted the rather unpleasant task of sheeting home responsibility. I said at the outset that it would be quite inappropriate to direct attention upon the Wades and Day and that it would be more productive to focus upon the Council and the Government who were responsible for making the system work. It may be convenient here if I reiterate why I felt those bodies should bear responsibility.

State Government Responsibility

• The Planning Act is defective. There is no prescribed remedy in such circumstances for an aggrieved resident to have the permit reviewed, nor to make the Council accountable for wrong decisions, nor to prevent illegal works from proceeding.
• The permit revocation provisions are quite inadequate in that the aggrieved residents were the only ones who could not initiate revocation proceedings, and even if such proceedings were convened, they have no right of subsequent appeal to the Appeals Board, that right lying only with the permit holder, the alleged 'guilty party'. Nor is it satisfactory that the aggrieved parties have no right to be present and be heard at such a hearing.
• Government is responsible for the Planning Scheme, that 'paradise for lawyers', which introduced considerable uncertainty and time wasting into the case.

115

• The preceding Government appointed the Commissioners who via their delegated planning officer issued the invalid permit and then failed to revoke it. An elected Melbourne City Council, with its tight committee review processes, would have been most unlikely to have issued such a permit and even if it had, it would certainly thereafter revoke any such permit once Councillors became fully informed of the proposal. Governments must surely be responsible for the actions of Commissioners—even if they are appointed by their predecessors.

• The administration of justice had failed to dispose of the matter expeditiously and there had been conflicting judicial pronouncements. It was the combination of these things which, it may be argued, proved fatal to the residents and increased the costs.

• By failing to acknowledge its vital role in the administration of the town planning and judicial processes the Government has failed to display those leadership qualities which could have resolved the matter at an early stage. There have been plenty of other occasions where it has been active in settling complex disputes. A more responsive Government would have recognised the deficiencies in the system and endeavoured to assist in resolving a settlement rather than ignoring the problem which only became more acute as a consequence.

• Not only did the Government refrain from taking a positive role but it has successfully blocked the Council from making reparation when the Council indicated a willingness so to do.

Council Responsibility

• Maladministration and lack of adequate procedures had led to the issue of an invalid permit.

• The consistent lack of co-operation, non-information and unsympathetic responses in the early stages compounded the difficulties and closed avenues by which the dispute could well have been resolved.

• The Council must also accept some responsibility for the actions of the Commissioners where the Government will not. Prima facie, it is responsible for those who suffer as a result of wrongful decisions made by Commissioners, Councillors and officers whether or not they are legally liable.

The Council has come to recognise its moral responsibility to its not inconsiderable credit.

A Public Issue

On the 12 June 1985, the Council passed a resolution stating that it was:

> . . . deeply concerned at the emotional and financial effects of the litigation over Number 17 Fitzgibbon Street Parkville, on all the parties involved.
>
> The core of the problem was the unfortunate legislative omission to build into the Town and Country Planning Act 1961 adequate safeguards to enable all potentially aggrieved persons to challenge the issue of a permit. Now that all litigation has ended, the Council will turn its attention not only to securing legislative amendments to prevent such a situation recurring . . . but also to obtaining substantial financial relief for the residents by direct contribution from the State Government'.

The case gained considerable momentum as a public issue after the appeal hearing when the *Age* weighed in again with a feature article by Tim Colebatch, A LEGAL DISPUTE WORTHY OF A DICKENSIAN PLOT. Colebatch started off by referring to the case of *Jarndyce v. Jarndyce* in Dickens' *Bleak House* — a case which had continued for two decades until it was realised that the costs had exhausted the assets of the estate! Colebatch neatly explained how in the Wade house case, innocent residents had suffered as a consequence of court delays, how the judge had found that the permit was invalid, and in a critical passage, that 'no reasonable responsible authority' could have decided the matter like this:

> . . . the courts in fact added to the problems . . . had they heard the matter speedily in 1982, a totally different outcome was likely.
>
> If the permit was ruled invalid and no building had begun, almost certainly the Wades would have been directed not to build but to seek a new permit. This would have enabled the effect on the neighbours to be properly debated in the Planning Appeals Board.
>
> Instead we had a ridiculously long delay . . . death of a crucial witness (which may well have affected the outcome), different judges giving different rulings on vital points — and absolutely immense costs.

Justices O'Bryan and Gobbo were furious. This was tantamount to criticism. They briefed Jack Winneke, QC, to represent them and conferred with the Chairman of the Bar Council, Alex Chernov, QC, who prepared an article for publication. The *Age* declined to publish the article despite a deputation to the Editor Creighton Burns. Lawyers have been puzzled as to why Justices O'Bryan and Gobbo should have been so sensitive. Perhaps it was a concern that the public might believe they were personally responsible for the errors which caused much of the tragedy. The *Age* stood firm and refused to publish the lengthy article written by Chernov but did publish a letter of Chernov's on 8 June to which was added an Editor's note. This conceded one error but went on to declare:

> For the rest, we reject Mr Chernov's accusations and stand by our article.
>
> The core of the case was whether or not the Wades had the right to build the sunroom. Mr Justice O'Bryan ruled that, through no fault of their own, they did not, because the Council had not considered the room's detrimental impact on its neighbours before issuing the permit. Thus is is true to say the residents won their point.
>
> Readers of his judgement can decide for themselves whether, when discussing what remedies should be granted, he placed equal weight on being fair to each side.
>
> Mr Chernov's account of the hearing before Mr Justice Gobbo is flatly contradicted by those present and by the available records . . .

The *Age* was unrepentant! Chernov, however, was able to find a vehicle in the barristers' bulletin, the *Victorian Bar News* and his article was published in the Winter 1985 issue. I have at times adverted to some of his comments in the course of this work but unfortunately space prevents a detailed summary and response. He claims, for example, that the residents should have initially acted with greater speed to get the matter into court; that the sunroom was substantially complete at the time of the issue of an injunction; that the residents did not press for an injunction, and that if they had 'His Honour would have heard argument from counsel and made a decision'; that the residents were responsible for court delays and the delays cannot fairly be laid at the feet of the Court; that it is wrong to create the impression that there were inconsistent decisions between two judges; that the basis of the case is alleged non-disclosure, misrepresentation and fraud; that it is a misleading summary (by Mr Colebatch), that the Court '. . . gives no protection once a neighbouring development has been permitted without their knowledge'.

I had gone to see Chernov at an early stage. I found him very civil and direct. However, it became apparent to me when I checked his information that he was ill-informed and had clearly relied upon second-hand comment. I was very disappointed by his article which is unworthy of a person of his fine intellect. While there is not room to undertake a point by point analysis here, hopefully the same journal will publish my response which will be duly forwarded.

There was, however, no let-up for the profession and an article in the *Herald* on 27 May 1985, by Kim Lockwood, analysed how the costs had escalated. It explained how one party will brief a Queen's Counsel which normally means that the other parties feel compelled to follow suit. A QC means a junior barrister must also be acquired which then means you are thinking in terms of up to $3000 a day. Court delays meant changing barristers, briefing and de-briefing witnesses, etc. The costs associated with the documentation proved incredible. The mandatory transcript fee was about $1000 a day and on top of this, the parties were required to pay a total of $12 per page—there were 2500 pages—a total cost of $30,000! It was explained that to mount an appeal you are required to provide an 'appeal book' which involves some antiquated methods. The appellant has to provide all the other parties and all of the judges with copies which cost another $25,000!

Thorne explained the residents' feelings:

> . . . people asked why we were proceeding with such big costs facing us. But when we started it seemed such an obvious matter. There had been an error made by the Council, and the judge found they had breached the Act.
>
> So we had to keep going, because we knew we were right.
>
> The judge found we were right, that a major error had occurred, that the Council had granted an invalid permit. But because the Wades had built in good faith nothing could be done about it.

Thorne said that he was not so much bitter as amazed that ordinary people should be forced to take such steps, that the costs were beyond ordinary people's reach and that the 'average citizen has no way of putting right an illegal act done by a public body'. He expressed concern at the 'Wades win' atmosphere whereas in fact the Wades, like them, had suffered 'enormous financial strain and stress over three years'.

Kim Lockwood set out the bill for the case:

The bill for the Wade Case

Plaintiffs' costs	City Council's costs	The Wades' costs
One QC at $2000 a day for 34 days: $68,000	One QC at $2000 a day for 34 days: $68,000	One barrister at $1300 a day for 24 days: $31,200
One QC's junior at (say) $1300 a day for 34 days: $44,200	One QC's junior at (say) $1300 a day for 34 days: $44,200	One QC at $2000 a day for 10 days: $20,000
Solicitors at $1000 a day for 34 days: $34,000	Solicitors at $1000 a day for 34 days: $34,000	One QC's junior at $1300 a day for 10 days: $13,000
Transcript of first case: $10,000	Transcript of first case: $10,000	Solicitors at $1000 a day for 34 days: $34,000
Preparation of 'Appeal Book' $30,000	Solicitors' fees for three years: (say) $100,000	Transcript of first case: $10,000. Solicitor's fees for three years: (say) $100,000
Solicitors' fees for three years: (say) $100,000	Stamp duties, phones, letters, other, for three years: (say) $5000	Stamp duties, phones, letters, other, for three years: (say) $5000
Stamp duties, phones, letters, other, for three years: (say) $5000		
TOTAL: $291,200	TOTAL: $261,200	TOTAL: $213,200

GRAND TOTAL
$765,600
To be met by the plaintiffs ($191,400 each)

Thorne expressed the feelings of a wide cross-section of the community when he commented, 'Nobody has won except the Council, the State Government and the legal profession'.

The case was further ventilated on television and in other articles. Crispin Hull in the *Canberra Times* in an article, WHEN THE LEGAL SYSTEM NO LONGER DELIVERS THE GOODS,[1] pointed out that it is cheaper to throw rights away than attempt to enforce them. He maintains that it is the rule, not the exception, that people cannot fully exercise their rights through fear of legal costs. He referred to the case of *Comalco v. the ABC*, in which Comalco was awarded $295,000 damages for defamation. The costs were estimated to be in excess of $2 million, and the appeal has not yet begun! Many lawyers in Melbourne are finding increasingly that clients are not prepared to risk litigation for fear of escalating costs. Julia Bruce, one of Melbourne's leading town planning lawyers wrote recently, 'If the Order Nisi procedures . . . took six weeks instead of up to 18 months to produce a result, the big delaying actions would be futile . . .'[2]

Yet another highly critical article appeared in the *Herald*, HIGH STAKES MAKE LAW A GAMBLE, where Kim Lockwood adverted to the Wade case and asked at the outset whether, 'the average person can afford to protect his or her rights'. He cited Gordon Lewis, Executive Director of the Victorian Law Institute as saying that going to court is 'like going to the races. You have to be able to afford to lose'. Mr Lewis says that the price of enforcing one's legal rights is not beyond the very poor (who may receive legal aid), or the very rich, but suggested that 'things are getting out of hand . . . for middle bracket income earners'. He also pointed out that leading silks earn more than $400,000 a year nett while even a 'great number . . . who are mediocre . . . still charge $1400 to $1500 a day'.

Mr Lewis, who not unnaturally has the solicitors perspective at heart, rubbed salt into the barristers wounds by adding that they normally charged more than solicitors despite the fact that the time expended was less and their overheads, 'as low as 15 per cent compared with the solicitors' 75 per cent'.

On 17 June, Phil Opas, QC, wrote to the *Age* outlining the procedures by which such cases could come before the Appeals Board and explained they were expeditiously dealt with, normally in 'six weeks'. He omitted to mention that the residents in the Wade house case had had no right of access to the Board. I believed his letter could confuse to the extent that people might believe that an appropriate remedy was not pursued. My response was published on 26 June:

> The difficulty was that *only* the council may initiate action to revoke the permit and *only* the permit holder can thereafter take the matter to the Board. Accordingly, in the Wade case, there was *no* access to the Board to remedy the invalidity, and *no* remedy other than to seek (protracted and cripplingly expensive) redress before the Supreme Court.
>
> Thus the law requires amendment since in the real world, it simply soes not make sense to expect a Council to admit wrong-

doing with alacrity nor for the holder of an alleged invalid permit to voluntarily allow review of the same.

It was about this time that replies from various Government ministers were being received stating that the litigation was a private action, that the Government would neither accept responsibility nor propose legislation to enable the Council to pay costs 'other than those awarded by the Courts'. One had the distinct impression that the Government firmly believed that the problem would go away if only they ignored it long enough. Recipients were advised, however, that Ministers were concerned that the Act 'should provide the best possible statutory framework for the functioning of the planning system' and that written submissions outlining suggested improvements, 'will be taken into account by a working group which has been set up'.[3] At last we thought, the Government is beginning to recognise that there is a problem even if little concern has been shown for the victims to date.

The National Trust took up the matter and on the front page of its bulletin said that, 'It is also clear that the innocent victims of this excruciating litigation, who sought to uphold the law and protect their homes, should now be compensated on a fair and equitable basis'. In a powerfully worded feature article in its July issue of *Trust News*, the Trust pointed out that citizens' rights to participate in planning had been whittled away and that,

> Henceforth, a Council wishing to steer a permit through for an abattoir, brothel, etc., whether for reasons of negligence, corruption or sheer contempt for citizens' rights, may ignore the perceived obligation to inform local residents.

The Government stood firm, despite hundreds of letters expressing concern from the public at large, resolutely refusing to even discuss the matter. In over three years since the dispute arose, the Minister for Planning, Evan Walker, has not once discussed the matter with the residents. To be fair, other parliamentarians such as Keith Remington and Gerry Hand have been supportive and discussed the matter with them.

The Government appeared to be totally unmoved. The legal profession continued to smart under the continuing criticism. Creighton Burns capitulated to the legal establishment eventually by publishing a comment, if not exactly an apology, at least indicating that the purpose of the article had been to 'canvass the question of whether the processes of the law were entirely adequate to cope expeditiously and within reasonable cost with legal disputes of this type . . . it was never its intention to cast any adverse reflection upon the capacity or integrity of Mr Justice Gobbo or Mr Justice O'Bryan or to impugn the manner or fairness in which they have respectively dealt with the issues . . .'[4]

The subject was further ventilated in the June issue of SPACE produced by the Town and Country Planning Association. It contained an article by the writer dealing with the planning and legal issues and there were other references to the case by various writers. The publication focussed upon the history and operation of the Planning Appeals Board. A letter from Sir Rupert Hamer which was reproduced in that journal is worth publishing for its lucid and practical approach:

> . . . The real trouble in the present case is that, because of a gross error by a planning authority, two sets of quite innocent parties are brought into conflict. In the circumstances I would think that the judgement of Mr Justice O'Bryan was quite right, and that the subsequent Appeal to the Full Court was ill-advised; but the real crux of the matter is—who should rightly bear the legal costs? And in this case it should clearly be the Melbourne City Council. The Act should be amended at once to make it possible for the Town Planning Appeals Board, or the Supreme Court, to order the payment of the costs of all parties where it is clearly shown to have acted improperly.
>
> These two amendments would restore equity in cases such as this, and uphold the original intentions of the Parliament in providing a cheap and accessible forum for ordinary citizens affected by planning proposals and decisions. Needless to say, the amendments should authorise the proposed 'ex gratia' payment by the Melbourne City Council to bring about some element of justice in the Wade case.[5]

Recent efforts by the Planning for Democracy Group have included exploring avenues by which the Council might legally be capable of resolving a settlement with the residents. Current legal opinion holds the view that the Council does not at present have the power to make such a payment.

The legal establishment remained resentful of the publicity

and growing unease with the profession. This was in the context of three judges being charged with criminal offences. Two were convicted, including Justice Murphy, a member of the highest court in the land—a conviction without precedent. Barristers had been accused of avarice and of accepting briefs regardless of their lack of expertise and the Commonwealth Ombudsman, Professor J. Richardson, recently pointed out that '. . . our legal system is dogged by delays and inefficiencies of administration . . . the superior courts are so costly to the average citizen that he does not use them'. He referred to our judiciary as 'autocratic and unaccountable'. One solution suggested by him was the appointment of an Ombudsman for Judicial Administration.[6]

The Council's attitude became increasingly receptive. At its last meeting before the election, in August 1985, it heard a deputation from the residents, the Wades and the Democracy in Planning Group. At its next meeting on 20 August it resolved to pay full or part compensation to the Wades and the objecting residents provided the Government would amend the legislation enabling this to be done.

As I write, the *Age* reported on 30 October 1985, that the Premier has stated that the matter will be investigated by the Government which is the most encouraging news the residents have received for a long long time. The announcement appears to be quite contrary to a letter received by the residents from Jim Simmonds, Minister for Local Government, where he claims that to empower councils to make such payments could facilitate gifts being made and this would be a most unfortunate precedent and accordingly there was no point in discussing the matter.

Obviously, of course, *ex gratia* payments can be made in an orderly fashion and if necessary, they could be subject to the consent of the Minister. It is difficult to understand Simmonds' viewpoint.

Footnotes

1 Crispin Hull, *Canberra Times*, 2 June 1985, p. 2.
2 SPACE, Journal of the Town and Country Planning Association, Melbourne, June 1985, p. 15.

[3] Letter from Jim Simmonds, Minister for Local Government, to the author, 1 July 1985.
[4] The *Age*, 4 July 1985.
[5] Letter from Sir Rupert Hamer to the author, 18 June 1985.
[6] Professor Jack Richardson, 'Lawyers should make more use of administrative channels', *Australian Law News*, June 1985, pp. 18–19.

Courtesy *Melbourne Times*

7
Overview

Of course the law is ludicrous but that doesn't mean there is
anything funny about it.

Barbara Falk

Houses for sale. Houses for sale.

Doug Wade

Our history has shown how the Wades came to South Parkville
and into conflict both with the residents and the Council over
a variety of issues. In relation to the front of their house, they
failed to obtain the necessary planning permits and when
brought to account, persisted with plans which were quite
unsympathetic to neighbourhood sensibilities. The dispute
was expeditiously resolved by the Appeals Board.

With regard to the rear, we saw how the tragi-comedy of
errors began when the Commissioners issued an invalid
permit and then failed to revoke it. The Wades continued to
build as quickly as they could, whenever they could. The
revocation proceedings proved ineffectual and consequently
the Government has established a Committee to consider
amendments to the law which alas, will be of little comfort to
the residents who have been financially ruined. It is claimed
that to increase opportunities to challenge permits would
create extensive litigation concerning the validity of permits
for major shopping centres. I find it difficult to believe that
such a problem cannot be solved. In any event, we can live
with ten developers engaging in their own litigious con-

frontations if this will enable one innocent person to protect his home and call a halt to illegal building which may be a 'disaster' for him.

Other solutions could serve to minimise the advent of cases like the Wade house case. Increased requirements for advertising and/or notifying residents of developments would largely solve the problem. Why, when such developments are largely irreversible, should there be so much secrecy?

The litigation dragged on and on through the courts with consequent complications and cost escalations. Judges made conflicting statements and two fundamental errors, court records proved inadequate and Justice Gobbo's assurances proved ineffectual.

The judges were at their best while dealing with the technical legal issues and some murky areas of the law have been resolved. But in relation to the non-legal and town planning issues, where they lacked experience and training, they got into difficulties and were clearly influenced by their own conservative value judgements especially concerning so called street 'demonstrations' and public participation. It was in this context that Justice O'Bryan exercised his discretion with such unfortunate consequences in relation to costs.

The Full Court did little to advance our understanding of the issues involved save for its pronouncements concerning the question of private rights—namely, that in this area we don't have any. It was not their role to judge the correctness of Justice O'Bryan's decision but to conclude whether he had been 'unreasonable or plainly unjust'. Justice O'Bryan was acquitted. The conservative attitudes of all four judges may be contrasted with those of Stuart Morris who made no value judgements of the parties involved although he finds the architect Norman Day, who might have been expected to anticipate problems, to have been, 'misleading and disingenuous'. Unfortunately, the rigorous analysis of Morris was not available to Justice O'Bryan when he tackled the complexities of the case.

The Appeals Board decision contrasts vividly with those of the Supreme Court. The former provided a relatively informal arena where costs could be controlled, procedures were simplified and matters dealt with relatively quickly. The

Court on the other hand, proved a nightmare from everyone's point of view — save perhaps for the lawyers. It may be argued that an issue such as misrepresentation could not be heard before an Appeals Board. In the first place, if the residents could have got their case on quickly before the Board, they would have gladly dropped the claim of misrepresentation. Secondly, as the lawyer Roger Batrouney has suggested, it may be that the Board needs to be re-structured with a more senior Chairman heading a division who could dispose of such legal issues in addition to planning issues. I do not pretend to know the perfect solution but I cannot believe that there is no scope for improvement.[1]

To its credit, the City Council has resolved to pay some reparation to the parties. The State Government remains impervious to suggestions that it has any responsibility. For some time Ministers have responded to enquiries with pro forma letters, reiterating that the case is one of 'private litigation' and that it would have been wrong for Government to be involved and that it will not amend the legislation to assist the Council to make reparation. The Ministers don't seem to have grasped what the judges actually said, namely that it was not 'private litigation', but public town planning rights that we are concerned with. The Act, it was held, does not confer private rights.

Clearly the town planning processes failed to operate adequately, clearly the legislation and Planning Scheme were defective, clearly the original issuing and failure to revoke the invalid permit was the fault of Government appointed Commissioners. Who but the Government should be responsible for these things? Initially we find the Minister for Planning, Evan Walker, seriously concerned and he, 'expects to be involved in the resolutions of the dispute at some stage and may be involved in court proceedings in connection with the property'.[2]

Very properly, Walker was concerned that the planning processes were failing to cope and hoped that he might resolve the problem. Something happened to change his mind and I can only suspect it was a cabinet decision which bound him to a hands off approach. Suddenly, all Ministers were responding to correspondence with pro formas reiterating the claim that it was 'private litigation' and that it would be wrong for the

Government to be involved. Even if it were 'private litigation', which it was not, that would not alter the fact that the problem arose and was compounded due to the faulty planning and judicial processes for which Government and Council are alone responsible. The argument has been put that if you choose to litigate, you get what you deserve—no matter how inadequate, apparently, the legislation may be and how unjust the decision may seem. It is of interest to note the recent litigation concerning the Nunawading by-election before the Court of Disputed Returns. The case was initiated by individuals, but like the Wade house case, was concerned with public issues and rights. The legal costs were borne by Government. *Through the Looking Glass?*

In the course of this tale I have refrained from repeating certain allegations which have circulated. Allegations have been rife but the laws of defamation are strict and prevent them from being aired here. Nevertheless, it is fair to say that many responsible and experienced people involved believe there is a great deal more that could, and in justice should be said about this whole affair.

The South Parkville community was confronted by a man who was insensitive to their neighbourhood aspirations and who, when he saw the ball within reach, believed in grabbing it and punting it goalwards, regardless of one or two opponents who might get in the way. The planning laws proved inadequate, the courts didn't function properly and the politicians became indifferent.

That is almost the end of the saga save for the final act. The bills are now coming home and the Wades' bill was recently costed by the Taxing Master for $102,121 and a writ taken out against the residents empowering the Sheriff to seize the residents' homes or property.[3] The Council's costs may be bigger still. The residents have now paid a total of $180,000 in legal costs and must find another $350,000 approximately. Since they cannot pay these bills the three families involved can now be forced to sell their homes. (The Notinis have been indemnified by the other residents and Dr Falk will not lose her home). Wade triumphantly declared that the first house to be seized would be number 19, belonging to Giovanni Notini, the shy, relatively defenceless septuagenarian Italian immigrant. It is sad that even now, Wade seems oblivious to the unseemly nature of his comments. After the appeal hearing, when it was obvious that the residents were in desperate financial straits, he taunted the Thorne children (Barbara and Michael aged 13 and 14) in the street with cries of 'houses for sale, houses for sale'.

Throughout the case the residents have asked, what more could they have done to protect their homes from the illegal development? They sought the best advice available and relied upon the courts to uphold the law and to protect them. Old fashioned notions concerning the rule of law and the courts being there to protect the innocent have taken a battering. True it is that a tactical error was made and with hindsight, the charge of misrepresentation should have been dropped. But can it honestly be said that justice requires that these families should now bear almost the total costs while the Council, which created and compounded the initial problem, should get off virtually scot free? I cannot believe this to be a just decision.

The only important issue remaining then is the question of moral responsibility. Will the Cain Government continue to assert that the problem doesn't exist, that it was simply a case of 'private litigation' and that if they repeat this often enough, it will all go away? Or will they come to terms with the notion of responsibility as did the Council, and assist the victims of these 'tragic circumstances' (to use the Minister's phrase)—or at the very least, stop blocking the Council from making a fair and just settlement which it now properly seeks to do?

Footnotes
[1] Our Sydney friends have been astonished by the case and lawyer John Mant commented in the September issue of SPACE, Journal of the Town and Country Planning Association, Melbourne, 1985:

The horrific tale of the *Wade Case* proves yet again the need in Victoria for a broad based Environmental Court modelled on the lines of the New South Wales Land and Environment Court. The *Wade Case* just could not have happened in New South Wales. At the first suspicion that a permit may have been issued invalidly, any of the residents could have taken Class 4 proceedings in the Court. A simple form and a two page affidavit would have obtained an interim injunction immediately. The Chief

Judge would have listed the hearing within a few days if the parties so wished. In my experience of proceedings in the New South Wales Court, a case such as *Wade*, if caught at the early stage, would have been completed in two, maybe three hearing days and within three months of having been commenced.

[2] Letter from Dr Michael Henry to Loretta Forsey, 23 August 1982, in which he explains the Minister's position and rebuts the claim made by Norman Day to have influence with the Minister.

[3] The *Herald*, 24 October 1985.

Postscript

One part of the saga is drawing to a close. On Saturday 9 November 1985 the Wade house was offered for sale at a forthcoming auction. Apparently overshadowing is not a problem in this 'highly sought after quiet street', the house being advertised as 'capitalising on full natural light'.

Courtesy the *Age*.